# WHAT OTHERS ARE SAYING ABOUT
## *THE TENDERNESS OF JESUS*

I am so thankful for this book. As someone who has experienced church and family trauma, it is hard not to lose hope and it is not always easy to remember the Lord of the church when the church feels disappointing or worse. In *The Tenderness of Jesus*, Rob speaks to the reader as a gracious dad speaks to his kids about the kindness and wonder of the person of Jesus. Our society is longing for real encounter, and people are still intrigued by Jesus. But, what do you do when those who bear his name cause pain? First, you can turn your eyes to Jesus and remember His love, His grace, and His tender invitation to relationship and transformation. I am hopeful that this book will speak to people on a wide spectrum of faith journey, and for those who feel disillusioned, I trust this is a warm welcome back to the open arms of a Savior who is better than we could possible imagine.

—**Tim Meier**
*Vice President for Development, The Alliance*

Oh, the beautiful heart of Jesus! I felt the tender love of Christ radiating from within these pages. Dr. Rob has so eloquently described a love that is indescribable. As I read these words I felt the heavy yoke of perfectionism falling away and God's grace and mercy resting upon me.

I am so often moved by the intimacy Dr. Rob shares with Jesus, and once again my spirit has been stirred. My heart was filled with a deeper yearning to know Jesus and a greater yearning to be His hands and feet in this broken world.

This book has fanned the flame within me, and I know it will set many other hearts ablaze and, at the same time, will burn away the things that hinder people from truly knowing just how wide and deep the love of Christ is for them. This book will touch many hearts, and I am blessed to be one of them.

—**JENNIFER TOSCANO**
*Writer,* A Heart Full of Hope

I've read all of my friend Rob's books. Each time I do, I think: this is the best one yet. This time I know I'm right. I really needed this word on the tenderness of Jesus. We have all been through a difficult season and I believe this amazing book written to Rob's children is a "NOW" Word for all of us. Thank you buddy!

—**RON WALBORN**
*VP and Dean of Alliance Theological Seminary*

*The Tenderness of Jesus* is without question a biblical, personal, and practical book about Christ. What makes it especially compelling is the intimacy with which the author writes about the Lord. Rob does not stand at an objective distance and dispense interesting facts about the life of Jesus. He opens his heart to us, sharing deeply moving encounters that he has had with the living Jesus. One can sense his passion as Reimer invites the reader into an intimate encounter with the tenderness of Jesus. Clearly, Rob Reimer has proven once again that he is a Jesus guy!

—**TERRY WARDLE**
*Author and Founder of Healing Care Ministries*

Encountering the tenderness of Jesus is greatly needed particularly for those who don't know Him and for those who need to reencounter Him. Dr. Rob has given a valuable resource for those struggling to see the goodness of God and the tenderness of Jesus. In this book Dr. Rob has brought biblical truth, applicable principles, and personal insights. He writes as one who has pursued and wrestled with God and found keys to encountering Jesus and shares insights on how to inspire and encourage others to do so. This work challenges and encourages us to that deeper journey with Jesus. It is for the leader, teacher, student, preacher, or proclaimer of faith in Christ.

—**REV. KEN GRAHAM**
*Regional Coordinator, Asia Pacific Region, Alliance World Fellowship and President, Christian and Missionary Alliance of Australia*

I had the privilege of reading this book in the weeks leading up to Easter, which gave it power and meaning I had not expected. I believe God as a loving Father orchestrated the timing as a gift giving me a deeper understanding and a renewed appreciation of the tenderness of Jesus.

In his book Rob interweaves both biblical knowledge and his own life story to bring us a compelling picture of who Jesus is and can be in our lives today. Rob, through his open, personal style, draws us in and invites us to see and experience Jesus as he has, "the most compelling, most beautiful, most tender person" we can and will ever know.

—**JOHN HUTCHINSON**
*Executive Minister, Churches of Christ, Western Australia*

"Pain subsides, life will end. But the tenderness of Jesus lasts forever."

*The Tenderness of Jesus* is the truth for which this generation has been waiting. They've been let down by leaders at home, at school, and in power. They've inherited a neutered church. They've been assailed by weaponized religion. They're burned out from striving and numbed out from soothing the void. They're hungry for authenticity, integrity, humility. They are ravenous for world change.

Who will save them?

There is only One whose shoulders can bear the burden they've carried and redeem it. His name is Jesus.

In *The Tenderness of Jesus* Dr. Rob Reimer doesn't speak as a man who has stood behind a pulpit, but as a father who has rocked his children in the midnight hour. He speaks as a dad whose heart bursts with love for his disquieted babies. To his kids he offers compassion, even amid rebellion, as he narrates his own transparency and accountability. In writing from this perspective as a loving father, Rob himself reflects Christ's love for His children. And as he releases them to their own paths in a tumultuous time, Rob points them toward True North.

*The Tenderness of Jesus* is a love letter from a father to his children. And we, as the reader, have the privilege of appropriating that story for ourselves.

Jesus Himself is the author and finisher of all the things we hope for and don't yet see. It's been said that He has selected and saved this particular generation to establish His plan for redemption. Bruised in a fallen world, He'll use their tenderness to carry it out. And he'll use *The Tenderness of Jesus* to show them how.

—**Elizabeth Hopkins**
*Journalist*

In *The Tenderness of Jesus,* Dr. Rob Reimer walks us through the process of understanding why a loving God would allow evil in our world. Jesus is God's solution to all the issues of humanity, and in this book, you'll understand just how much so. He brings us back to the fundamentals, focusing our eyes on Jesus and Him alone. Dr. Rob illustrates the beauty that can be found through the goodness of Jesus and His sacrifice for the sake of a broken world. The reminders and examples of the true tenderness of Jesus spilled on these pages will reignite a tenderness in yourself toward the Father and toward those around you. I invite you to read this book and encounter Jesus as He really is, perhaps as you have never known Him before.

—**Ron Eivaz**
*Senior Pastor, Harvest Church (harvestonline.church)*
*and Founder and Apostolic Overseer, Harvest Ministry*
*Network (hmnetwork.org)*

In *The Tenderness of Jesus,* we get to experience family as Rob lovingly describes to his four children what Jesus is like. Drawing from his own years of walking with Jesus, Rob candidly shares family stories as a beautiful reminder of God's deep love for us demonstrated in the person of Jesus. A must read!

—**Dr. Wanda Walborn**
*Author of* Spiritual Journey, Can I Really Get Close to God?, *Associate Professor of Spiritual Formation at Alliance Theological Seminary*

With the heart of the Father, Dr. Rob Reimer speaks to the will and to affections of people who long for the authentic with God and community. The approach is fresh; the insight profound; the tenderness heartfelt. Read it for yourself and those you love!

—**DR. MARTIN SANDERS**
*Global Leadership, ATS*

# The Tenderness of Jesus:

*An Invitation to Experience the Savior*

## Dr. Rob Reimer

Carpenter's Son Publishing

Published by Carpenter's Son Publishing, Franklin, Tennessee

Interior Design by Suzanne Lawing

Cover Design by Danielle Reimer

Edited by Robert Irvin

Printed in the United States of America

ISBN: 978-1-956370-02-7

# ACKNOWLEDGMENTS

So much to be grateful for, so many people to give thanks to. I am grateful for all the people who have helped contribute to this book. I am grateful to my daughter Darcy for the conversation that ultimately gave birth to the idea of writing *The Tenderness of Jesus*, and for designing the cover for this latest work of mine (as she has done for several other books). I am grateful to you, Jen, for being a constant source of goodness in my life and a gift of God to me for 33 years of marriage! If I could do it all over, I'd choose no one else but you. And to all the rest of the children—Danielle, Courtney, and Craig, and for more recent additions to our family, Chris, Sam, and Caius—I am glad God put all of you in this family with me. You're a joy!

I am grateful for Bob, Larry, and Shane for your help with the process of producing yet another book.

I am grateful for all the people who have demonstrated Jesus' tenderness to me and others over the years—family, friends, teachers, pastors, lay people, and other writers. I needed to see it, hear about it, and experience it from people like you.

Thank you to all of you who took your time to endorse this volume for me. Your time and your words are a gift to me, and I greatly appreciate you taking the time to read it and write about it.

And to those of you who have read the books I write—I am truly grateful. Thank you for the encouragement, feedback, and testimonies of life change that you have shared with me over the years. I have been deeply touched by all of it more than you know.

# DEDICATION

To Jesus: You simply are the most beautiful, most compelling, most tender person who ever lived. I surrendered my life to you at nineteen and I have never once regretted that decision or looked back on it with anything but gratitude. Thank you, Jesus, for your overwhelming, transforming, healing, and consoling tenderness. Your presence and kindness have marked my journey, changed my life, and saturated my existence with eternal significance and hope. All the way through writing this book I found myself in tears because of my personal experience with your tender love. I am still completely captured by you. If I had one thousand lives to live, I'd live them all for you.

# CONTENTS

# PREFACE
## Please Read This First

Dear reader, first of all, if you have read my other books, I want to thank you. I greatly appreciate your readership and loyalty to come back and read this my latest book. Often in conferences I have people approach me and tell me they have read all my books, and they talk about the impact they have made. I am grateful to you, and that is why I write—for me it is always about life change for the honor of Jesus.

Second, I want you to know that this book is going to be different than any other book of mine that you have read. What makes it unique is the voice with which I write. Normally I write my books directly to you, the reader. My style is direct, personal, practical, and vulnerable. In this book you will be listening to me speak directly to my adult children. My kids are 20, 23, 26, and 27 at the time of this writing. I am writing this book directly to them, so you will hear me writing as a dad to his grown-up kids—and I invite you to listen in. I am writing about the One who I love directly to these ones who I love.

I decided to write from this perspective because this book was inspired by a conversation I had with my third daughter, Darcy, and it felt appropriate to write it in this manner. I will tell you about that conversation in the Introduction. I also decided to write this way because, in some ways, it will feel even more personal. It is as if you are invited to sit around the dinner table with us and listen to me talk with my children about the most astonishing person I know. As you read, imagine sitting with us, listening to family banter and our reminiscing about our story and Jesus' story. Last, I used this voice because I want to leave this book to my children as part of their legacy and inheritance; not a monetary inheritance, a spiritual inheritance. This is the Jesus who I know and have experienced. No one has amazed me more, touched me deeper, or moved my heart with passion like Jesus has.

Ultimately, this is a story about Jesus and me and sometimes about Jesus and our family. He has been the most important person in my life for the past four decades, since I decided to go all in and follow Him and not just leave Him at the edges of my life. It was the best decision I ever made. I want my children to know Him as I have known Him, to love Him as I have loved Him, to encounter Him as I have encountered Him, and to follow Him as I have followed Him. I don't want my children, or you, to just know about Jesus, like we know about a historical figure we read about in the pages of history. I want them, and you, to know Him up close and personal, to be embraced by His transforming presence, to be revived by His tender love, and to experience Him in real, authentic, and tangible ways. That has been my journey with the risen Christ. I want my children, and you, to know why I have been so Jesus-centered, Jesus-enamored, Jesus-oriented, Jesus-focused. I want my children to catch a glimpse of the Savior through the eyes of their father, and I am inviting you to join us on the journey. When I am dead and graduated to Heaven, I want my children to have this book to look back on, to turn to and read and remember why I was who I was and why I did what I did, what motivated me and captured me for a lifetime. And you, dear reader, are invited into that unique opportunity of listening to a dad pass on his love for Jesus to the children he will always adore.

For both you and them, I pray that you would encounter Jesus on these pages. You won't just know about Him, you will experience Him in all His compelling glory, beauty, majesty, and tenderness. Long ago when I was in college, I heard a man give his testimony. He had no religious background. His family had never been to church; he knew nothing about God. But one day he was in a bookstore and picked up a Bible. He began reading from the beginning. He clearly saw the problem of sin in the ancient world and could see the parallel examples in our modern world. But more than that, he was feeling the weight of it in his own soul. As he came to the New Testament he became completely transfixed with the person of Jesus. He was amazed by Jesus' teaching, His miracles, and His tender compassion. But he saw this dark plot beginning to emerge in the text: there were people who hated Jesus and began plotting against Him. The man rushed forward to the end of the story and wept as Jesus died, and then he was amazed as Jesus rose to life again. He had no context for the story. Unlike so many of us, it wasn't an old, slightly tired, worn-out story, and familiarity hadn't bred contempt or indifference. His heart was utterly captured by Jesus Christ. He read the rest of the New Testament and made a decision that he would follow Jesus wholeheartedly. It has been almost forty years since I heard that man's testimony, but I never forgot it.

I think it stuck with me for a few reasons. First, I was amazed someone could grow up in America and have no knowledge of this story and be so surprised by it. Second, I envied him; I envied that ability to hear the story of Jesus for the very first time. It is like falling in love for the very first time. You feel things you have never felt before, and your heart is so full. It is like having a child for the first time; your heart expands in ways you never could have imagined. Only it is infinitely better than all of that because this Jesus is the God of the universe who loved you so much He would join the human family, enter a suffering world, and experience all the ups and downs of life with us and suffer for us on a cross so He would win our hearts back to God. It is an unparalleled event in human history; there is nothing else even remotely like it. But we get so used to hearing it that it no longer moves us like it should. And when I heard that man speak about his first encounter with Jesus, I just longed to encounter Him for the first time, all over again, as an adult. The newness, the freshness, the beauty, and the wonder of it all. Last, I think the story has stuck with me all these years because of that man's sheer love for Jesus. He was completely obsessed, totally ruined for all that earth has to offer. And this was because he didn't just know about Jesus, he had met the living Christ, experienced the weight of sin lifted away from his soul. He knew the power of Jesus to change a human heart.

Far too many who believe in Jesus get wrapped up in all sorts of things that don't matter in the light of eternity. They lose their way while sidetracked by life, its worries, its hardships, and its heartaches. They get lost in the spiritual woods looking for earthly treasures or temporal pleasures. They get hurt and offended by people and God and lose their way in life. In the end, the once passionate, burning love for Jesus that consumed them is lost, and some wander away from Jesus and the church while others stay the course and yet have lost their first love. This world has a way of trying to get all of us to take our eyes off of Jesus. But in my forty years of walking with Jesus, I have discovered that life works better when I have Jesus at the center of my heart, soul, and daily existence. I have found that when Jesus is my first love, and I have a firm grip on eternal realities, I don't lose my peace even in the darkest hours. And during life's more mundane and routine seasons I find this unmistakable joy and satisfaction in Jesus' presence and service.

So, for all of you, dear readers, my children, and my children's children (our first grandchild was born April 14, 2023), may you all come to know, experience, and fall in love with this Jesus who I know. There is no greater joy in life, there is no greater fulfillment, no deeper peace, no richer reward than following Jesus wholeheartedly. As you read, may you experience Him. May your hearts be captured, recaptured, renewed, and revived for the One who is tender and compassionate like no other.

*Rob Reimer*
*July 25, 2023*

Growing up with a father who knew and embodied the tender hospitality and inclusivity of Jesus wasn't always easy as a child. It was hard to share my father with a congregation, many of whom knew him intimately or even saw him as a father figure in their own life. As an adult I have come to cherish my father's insistence on including anybody who was willing to come to our figurative (and literal) dinner table discussions. This insistence has been a wonderful reflection of Jesus' desire to have a deeply personal relationship with each of us. I am proud to have inherited this same desire to embody the compassion and open arms of Jesus that my dad exemplified in our home, and I hope to pass it on to my own children.

My siblings and I would like to earnestly invite each of you to listen in to our dinner table chat and share in our spiritual inheritance bestowed upon us by our father, just as Jesus invites you to share in His heavenly inheritance bestowed by His Father. May you encounter the tenderness, hospitality, and inclusivity of Jesus through this book in an indelible, intimate, and life-changing way.

*Danielle Reimer, for the siblings*
*May 3, 2023*

*"To live on Christ's love is a king's life."*
—SAMUEL RUTHERFORD[1]

Introduction

# RECONSTRUCTION

I was on a trip to Hawaii with Jen and my daughter Darcy. Jen stayed back at the hotel so she could go swimming at the beach, but Darcy and I decided we would explore the northernmost tip of the Island. My daughter launched us into a great conversation with an intriguing question.

Darcy asked me, "Dad, why is that I love you and I love your faith, but I struggle with most Christians and their faith?" We were driving around the tip of Maui on a two-way road about as wide as a single-car driveway, and we spent five hours talking about the Bible and the tenderness of Jesus. It was that question, and that conversation, that inspired me to write this book.

While in Hawaii I had given a talk on the tenderness of Jesus, and Darcy asked me for book recommendations on the subject because she knew she needed to understand this tenderness, and it was hard for her to grasp. I looked at several books, but none of them addressed the kinds of things we had discussed in our conversation, and none of them were completely and entirely focused on Jesus. So I texted Darcy one night with a book that she might try, and then I wrote, "I think I'll write a book on the tenderness of Jesus for you." She wrote back, "I think that's a very good idea."

The more I thought about it, the more I realized there are many people out there like my daughter who are struggling with seeing the goodness of God and tenderness of Jesus. I am writing this book for all the wandering and lost sheep (to use Jesus' analogy) in hopes that it will help some find their way back to God amid all the spiritual haze created by a world full of evil. I'm writing it for all the people who could use a fresh encounter with the tenderness of Jesus to awaken their hearts for God and heal their souls.

I understand why people struggle with faith. There are many roadblocks, but there are two particularly large factors I want to address. These two factors are like two lenses that we often view God through, but like any lens, they color our understanding of reality. The two lenses that have distorted our view of God are the lens of evil in the world and the lens of the evil done by the people *in the church,* especially Christian leaders.

First, people struggle with faith because of the problem of evil. Our world has been undeniably and indelibly marked by the presence of evil. Much of the evil can be attributed to people's personal choices. Rape, abuse, violence, and other great harm has come into many of our lives because of the evil things that people choose. God created us in His image and, therefore, we have free choice. God is sovereign, and as image-bearers, it follows, we have been created with a degree of sovereignty, and that implies that we have choice, and we have authority. Choice to choose for good or bad; authority to overcome evil and the enemy of our souls. But sadly, too often, we use our freedom in ways that negatively impact others. Most of the evil in the world is explainable through human choices—not just on an individual level, but also on the grander scale. Whether it is war, the abuse of the environment, or corrupt and oppressive governments, this evil is ultimately the result of human choices. When I study the history of the world, it is hard for me to blame God for World War II, as an example. People made evil choices, and the world was left with dreadful consequences.

I once talked to a Jewish doctor, and I asked him about his faith. He responded, "After the Holocaust, who could believe?" But I have never understood blaming God for the evil that people perpetrate. The way I see it, if God was going to honor our right to choose, and He was not going to be the Dictator of the universe, then evil was going to permeate our world. His only option would have been to eliminate freedom, and then He would not have been good; He would have been an oppressor. So choice remained and evil resulted. You can either be evil and eliminate the choice of others or empower choice and allow for the possibility of evil. Human behavior explains so much of the problem of evil.

But there are things that cannot be explained by human choices—whether they include tsunamis or floods or earthquakes that kill thousands of people or certain diseases that ravage human life. To anyone who is an honest observer, it is obvious that the world is a broken place full of pain and hardship. It is clearly not a paradise. And the evil in our world is like a giant scratch on the lenses of our spiritual vision. I wear reading glasses, and sometimes they are so gummed up I can barely make out the words I am trying to read through the smudges. I am forced to stop and clean my lenses if I want to proceed with the work at hand. So it is that the evil in our world distorts our spiritual perception to see the goodness of God with great clarity. This is one of the reasons why Jesus came. He came to help us see clearly who God really is in all His goodness.

Second, people struggle with faith because the church has been marred by sinful people and religion. Too often people get focused on what other people do in the name of Jesus, rather than focusing on Jesus Himself. Recently, I was on a trip to England, and while wandering through the Cotswolds I was talking with a shop owner. She was a delightfully warm individual and asked me what I did for a living. I told her I was an author, had been a pastor, and that I wrote from a Christian perspective. She told me she struggled with God because of all the evil things that were done in the church. She spoke specifically about a recent revelation of sexual abuse in the church. I simply said to her, "Stories like this are terribly sad, and it represents Jesus so poorly. But don't make your decision about who Jesus is based on what people have done. Make it about Jesus. Not about the church, and not about people's evil choices. Let Jesus represent Himself; don't judge Jesus by people who represent Him poorly." She agreed that she needed to take a fresh look at Jesus and not judge him through the lens of the sins committed by people in the church, and she told me she would do so.

As for all the questions out there about the problem of evil: why does God allow this? Why doesn't God do anything about that? Jesus is God's ultimate answer. Jesus is the most compelling person I know. Jesus helps us cut through all the scratches and smudges on our lenses and see what God is truly like in the middle of a world distorted by evil. The author of Hebrews wrote: "In the past God spoke to our ancestors through the prophets at many times and in various ways, but in these last days he has spoken to us by his Son, who he appointed heir of all things, and through whom also he made the universe. The Son is the radiance of God's glory and the exact representation of his being, sustaining all things by his powerful word" (Hebrews 1:1-3).

God was trying to speak to us through our distorted lenses of evil and religion, but it was hard for us to have ears to hear and eyes to see. That is why Jesus came. God wanted to speak to us directly, so He entered our world. He became one of us. The Creator became as one of the created ones; He entered our material world and shared in our bodily experience. He suffered at the hands of evil people like all the rest of humanity who live in this dark, distorted, difficult world. He experienced the oppression of religion and its abuses like many of the rest of us—remember, it was religious people who falsely accused Jesus and put Him to death. He was tempted by evil, but not overcome by it. He was murdered on a cross and buried, but death could not keep Him down. No one could prove that Jesus was still dead by producing His body because the tomb was empty, and He lives. This is my greatest hope in a world of darkness. He came to show us who have been marred by evil what God is really like.

Jesus is the radiance of God's glory. He shines forth what God is like; He is a beacon of light that cuts through the darkness of evil and radiates the goodness of God to us. He is the exact representation of God the Father. If you want to know what God is like, look to Jesus. Don't look through the lens of evil or the lens of the church or religion. Look to Jesus. That is why Jesus came. The world is not an exact representation of God. The church is not an exact representation of God. Jesus is. He came to freshly present what the Father is like to those of us who are spiritually impaired by a world in suffering.

\* \* \* \* \*

Mostly, I am writing this book to you, my four children. As I write this in 2022 and 2023, you are all in your twenties, ranging from 20 to 27. And it seems to me that your generation has struggled more with your faith than those of my generation. There are likely many reasons for this. You are better informed about the problems of the planet than my generation was. Information is much more readily available due to the Internet, cell phones, social media platforms, and numerous news outlets. Thus, you are more sensitized to the pain and brokenness of the world than I was at your age. I don't know that ignorance is bliss, but I do know that an overload of the knowledge of evil can make us jaded and even cynical.

There has also been a significant shift in the role of the media. Think back to my grandparents' generation: President Franklin Delano Roosevelt was in a wheelchair and the media knew this, but they never presented it to the public. They kept it secret for the sake of the president. The fact that Roosevelt was in a wheelchair wasn't scandalous, but they protected the president; this would be unheard of today. They also knew of his sexual liaisons, as well as knowing the same about President John F. Kennedy and civil rights leader Martin Luther King Jr., both in the 1960s. But they covered those up as well. Again, that would never happen today. The media in our culture would do everything they could to expose a scandal—and sometimes even create one when it isn't true! When I was young, there undoubtedly was sexual abuse happening in the church, but no one talked about it or reported on it. Sadly, the church also covered it up—one of the evils committed by some church leaders. I can remember when the first sexual scandals were exposed in the church; it was shocking, but now this problem is all too common, and it has left many of us skeptical of nearly all things spiritual. Scandals get explored and exposed today, and we are now fed a steady diet of this unwholesome food. It severely undermines our trust in spiritual leaders and religious institutions, and we are left jaded.

There has also been a lot of legalism and religion in the church which has led to oppression and judgment. As a result, too often Christians have held to "the truth" with little or no grace—or at least their version of the truth. Many leaders in the church have mistakenly acted as if Jesus' number one command was to hold on to and fight for the truth rather than to love God and love people (Matthew 22:37). Too often the church has angrily stood against people who did certain things and acted certain ways. It has led to hurt, division, judgment, and, once again, left many people confused about what Jesus is really like. It was the Pharisees who represented this judgmental version of religion in the New Testament era. Sinners flocked to be with Jesus because they felt no judgment, only love. Tragically, too often the church today is more like the Pharisees than it is like Jesus. How we have missed the mark and misrepresented Jesus to so many!

Sometimes Christianity has been closely linked to politics, and again, this has confused the issue of Jesus. In my generation, right-wing politics and faith became nearly synonymous for some people. For some, to be Christian was to be Republican. But Jesus isn't a Republican, nor is He a Democrat. Sadly, now many people that I talk with who are against this version of Republican Christianity are simply rebelling against the religion of their parents by leaning left in the name of Jesus, and to be Christian for some now is to be Democrat. Is that really going to be any better? I have talked to some people in the inner city who can't understand how a Christian would vote Republican, and others in the suburbs who cannot believe a real Christian would ever vote Democrat. Personally, I would just like to get back to Jesus. Let's make it more about Jesus and less about politics, and let's not confuse Jesus with our political views. Let's make it more about Jesus and less about us.

There are also many people who have been hurt by various positions taken in the church. This, for example, includes women in ministry. At one point in my church in New England, I had the only two women pastors working in any church in the New England District of our denomination. When I hired a woman pastor for the first time, I didn't know it would be an issue. I had resolved the theological issues surrounding women in ministry before I became a pastor, and I didn't realize it was contentious until I received a phone call from the district office. It was the secretary who called me, and she asked, "What are you going to call Deb?" I had no idea why she was asking this question. I innocently answered, "Pastor Deb." She huffed this reply: "You can't call her Pastor Deb." I said, "Well, that's what we wrote in the bulletin, and that's what we are calling her. You can put whatever you want down on your denominational form, but we are calling her

Pastor Deb." I called the district superintendent afterward, and he was fine with it.

But, sadly, a lot of young women, including you, my three daughters, grew up in the church seeing that women were not treated as equals by the leaders of the church, and it has left many women feeling devalued. Jesus isn't like that. I know this has been hurtful to you, children, and I am sorry. Some of that inevitably led to resentment, not just against the church, but sometimes against Jesus. Once again, the attitudes and behaviors of the church put smudges on our spiritual lenses, and we confuse the theological positions of the church with the heart of Jesus.

The harshness of the world and the judgment of the church have distorted many people's views of the goodness of God and the tenderness of Jesus. One of the results is that there has been a lot of talk about "deconstruction" in the church. But as I listen to the deconstructionists, it is my observation that much of what is presented as deconstruction just ends up being destructive because there is no reconstruction. Too often the deconstruction ends up being destructive because it too closely associates Jesus with the church. We don't end up deconstructing the forms and practices of the church; we end up deconstructing Jesus, and what I have seen is that many times people are left with little to no faith at all. They construct Jesus in their own image, but they don't let Jesus represent God to them. They are left standing in a pile of rubble as if a bomb went off, and they are confused and concussed, and they don't know how to move forward. As I talk with people who stand in the spiritual rubble, I have to confess: they don't seem better off in life.

Listen, I am not defending the church. My calling is revival, and I believe the church needs to be revived and reformed. I am not pastoring anymore, and I attend a lot of different churches in my travels. Not long ago I was visiting a church, and as I was walking outside to the car afterward with Mom, I said to her, "The church isn't working; we need to change it." I wasn't referring to that specific church. In general, what we are doing in the church isn't working right now, and we need to reform our forms of church. We need to create new models, new paradigms, and new expressions of the church. We need a change of heart and a fresh visitation of the Spirit. We need to clean up judgment and oppression and represent Jesus well to a confused and concussed generation. But this is important: we must deconstruct the church without destroying the radiant glory of Jesus. We must change the church and some of our dogmatic opinions without destroying the revelation of who Jesus really is. We have to make it about Jesus and stop making it too much about people and about the church. We have to stop making it about our biases and our hurts, and truly make it about Jesus. Let Jesus speak for Himself; let Jesus represent God to us again. Let's take a fresh look at Jesus, who He is and what He is like, and not get completely sidetracked by the people who have represented Him poorly. If we are going to represent Jesus better to the next generation, it won't be because we are angry with how the previous generation misrepresented Him. Saying that people in the church are hypocrites and walking away from Jesus is a form of hypocrisy itself—we are judging Jesus by the people who have misrepresented Him, rather than allowing Him to be who He is. We need a people of God to rise up and represent Jesus well.

One of the things I've discovered about the hardships and sufferings of this world is that we need to separate life from God. This is what I mean: life is life and God is God. They are not the same thing. Life is harsh, cruel, painful, and all too often tainted by evil. But God is good. We will never see the goodness of God without a fresh look through the lens of Jesus' life. He is the exact representation of our good, heavenly Father. As we have to separate Jesus from the church, so we also must separate Jesus from the evil in the world. The church is broken, fallen, and led by sinful people who represent Jesus poorly, even on our best day. But Jesus is beautiful, whole, pure, tender, and compelling. I've said this before, but the biggest problem with the church today is that we are making it too much about us and not enough about Jesus. We are making it too much about our ideas, our wants, our needs, our feelings, and our opinions. We are supposed to follow Jesus; when the church is at its broken best, it is keenly focused on Jesus.

You, my daughters and son, know that our family history has a lot of sexual immorality, adultery, and the like. But Mom and I have been faithful to each other. I am part of our larger family, but I haven't made the same choices that some in my extended family have. I am a pastor and an author. There have been a lot of scandalous stories about pastors in the past couple of decades. But while I am like them in some ways, I have not made the same choices that some of them made. If someone views me through the lens of my family history or the lens of fallen church leaders, they will not see me for who I am. And, admittedly, I am deeply flawed. But in a similar way, we cannot look at Jesus through the lens of evil in the world or the lens of sin in church leaders without distorting who He is. We have to understand Jesus for Himself, and when we see Him for who He is, this can help us make sense of a lot of these other troubling things.

Too often when I am in a Christian gathering, the conversation is not about Jesus. The conversation is about church, life, current events, politics, and our opinions, but it isn't about Jesus. We are missing the main thing. God knew if we were going to understand Him, He would need to do something religion couldn't do. That's why Jesus came.

\* \* \* \* \*

In this book I am going to explore Jesus. I want to simply get back to Jesus. I am going to look at a couple of my favorite descriptions of Jesus, His compassionate interactions with people, and His tenderness through His parables and words. I am going to look, in a fresh way, at how Jesus shows us who God is and what He is like. I'll mix in some stories about how Jesus is still meeting people tenderly today. I invite you to open your heart to Jesus again. If you've been hurt by the church, if you've been hurt by religion, if you have been jaded by the evils of our world or all the stories of fallen Christian leaders, try to clear off the grime and smudges from your lenses and see who Jesus really is. There is no one like Jesus.

I want you to know that I too have struggled with understanding God's goodness. I began going to church when I was a toddler, and I started reading my Bible in my teen years. When I first read the Bible, I struggled with the problem of evil. I wrestled with why God didn't do more in some instances and why God did what He did at other times. I questioned the goodness of God.

But then I encountered Jesus when I surrendered my life to Him after a relationship breakup. I had a picture of Jesus standing in front of me; I could see his arms open wide, ready to embrace me, and I saw myself in the picture refusing his love. My heart broke over my rejection of this tender Man of Mercy, and I burst into tears of repentance and surrendered my life to Jesus. I said, "From now on, you lead, I'll follow. You've got me; I'm yours." And the tender love of Jesus came in like a flood. That encounter with Jesus' love and compassion changed everything for me. It didn't give me intellectual answers to all my questions, but it did give me authentic experience with the compassion of Christ. It didn't end all my struggles in life, but it did fortify my trust in the goodness of God. It didn't clean up all the problems in the world or the church, but it did clean my smudged glasses so I could see Jesus in all His beautiful, tender love.

I am writing this book for you, my four children: Danielle, Courtney, Darcy, and Craig. Therefore, I am going to write it as if I were writing to you personally, because I am. I am writing this book because of that conversation with Darcy in Maui, but I know she is not alone in her struggles to see God's goodness in a world like ours.

I am also writing this book for all of you who have struggled to keep a grip on the goodness of God in a world full of pain. I suspect there are many prodigal sons and daughters who would benefit from this book, many spiritual wanderers who can gain guidance in these pages, and many confused and concussed spiritual seekers who will benefit from a fresh glimpse of Jesus. I imagine that there are also many who are worn and weary because of the darkness of the world, and I hope this book will bring you refreshing as you encounter Jesus' kindness in a new and unique way. I pray this book will benefit all of you. I want all to know the tenderness of Jesus because it changes everything—it doesn't change the world around you in all its harshness, but it does change the world within you through all His tenderness. I won't answer all your questions or resolve all your dilemmas, but I hope to give you a fresh encounter with the One who came to represent the radiance of God's goodness to you. May you meet Jesus, as I have met Him, and may His tenderness heal your heart and reinforce your trust as it has mine.

\* \* \* \* \*

Imagine Jesus came to your house tonight simply to visit with you. He wasn't asking you for anything or telling you to do anything. He came just to be with you. What would your reaction be? Some of you would be nervous because you would think of the things you have done that you are not proud of, or even ashamed of, and sitting in the presence of Jesus would suddenly make you feel naked and exposed spiritually. Some of you would turn your nervous energy into trying to make everything just right—making sure the house is spotless, the food delicious, the presentation perfect. Like Martha, you would be distracted by the many things that had to be done. Some of you would be struck with sadness because your life would play before your eyes, and you would feel the weight of many wasted moments, frivolous activities, and temporal attachments. Some of you would feel anger because of the many unanswered questions in life; you would want to know why Jesus didn't intervene or help. But if we could get over our initial emotional reactions and just pay attention to Jesus, I suspect many of us would be moved to tears because we have never experienced such tender, overwhelming love.

If we could get past ourselves and fully attend to Jesus' presence, we would encounter a soul-stirring tenderness that awakens eternal longings deep within us. Jesus wouldn't need to say anything or do anything; just being with us would be more than enough. If we could just pay attention to His presence in our living room, we would sense that He has no judgment to offer for our many mistakes. He knows them all, but He holds nothing against you; He simply accepts you—flaws and all. Jesus did not come into the world to judge us, but to redeem us. If we could focus on Jesus, we would discover our nervous energy dissipate under His consuming love. He accepts you and loves you without any condition and beyond reason. If we could slow down our personal RPMs and focus on Jesus, we would discover a love that satisfies in a way all the temporal offerings of this world simply never have.

If you could get past yourself, and look into Jesus' eyes, and linger with Him, you would see a depth of love you have never encountered. It would simply move you to tears and draw you in. Never before have you met someone so compelling, so irresistible, so complete, so whole. As you sat in Jesus' presence and stilled your soul long enough to simply be with Him, you would feel the unmatched depth of His soul welcoming you into an emotional fullness that you have never experienced but always longed for. As you waited with Jesus, you would be overcome with longing—longing to be with Him and never leave Him, longing to be like Him and represent Him to others, longing to go with Him wherever He would lead you, longing to spend eternity with Him. No one stirs longing in my soul like Jesus because no one loves me with an untainted love like He does.

As Jesus sits with you in your living room, you observe that He carries a stillness and peace that is otherworldly. All the hurry, worry, busyness, and tension within your soul is swallowed up by His eternal peace. No words are spoken, but the world seems to stop on its axis, and everything becomes clear, if only for this moment. It is the presence of One who never gets overwhelmed with the temporal because He is so rooted in the eternal. It is the wisdom of One who never gets confused over what ultimately matters. He brings a simplicity and clarity to every confusing temporal situation.

As Jesus sits with you in your living room, you find tears spilling down your face. You don't even know why. Tears of unfulfilled dreams, unmet desires, unhealed pains, and heart-aches are drawn out by His healing presence. Quietly He reaches over and wipes away the tears from your eyes, and your soul is healed by His loving presence. Life has left its mark with hurts and scars that cannot completely heal until they are brought into Jesus' presence.

Imagine what it would be like to meet Jesus in your living room without the lens of religion or the lens of evil. He calms, stills, heals, restores, replenishes, redeems, fulfills, and satisfies. The tenderness of Jesus is what you would discover if Jesus came to your house tonight and sat in your living room. And you would discover that this is what your heart has always ached for.

In this book, it is my desire to help you, in one way or another, encounter Jesus in your living room. Don't rush past the moments the Holy Spirit affords. Linger with Jesus and let the longings of eternity be stirred in your soul by the One who loves like no one before.

*"Jesus Christ is the loveliest person souls can set their eyes upon."*

— John Flavel[2]

## One

# TENDER DESCRIPTIONS

*"To the lady chosen by God and to her children, whom I love in the truth"*

— the Apostle John (2 John 1)

Dear loved ones, I have walked with Jesus now for nearly four decades, and I can attest to His tenderness not merely through the witness of Scripture but also in my personal experience. I have met Jesus in my victories and in my defeats. I have encountered Him in some mountaintop experiences, and in the darkest, lowliest valleys. Jesus has walked beside me through fearful, anxious moments, and He has displayed His loving mercy to me when I have wandered from Him in anger, hurt, and sin. He has been a constant source of tenderness through it all. I only wish that everyone knew Him as I have experienced Him, and that is why I write to you.

I want to begin by focusing on a few passages that describe what Jesus is like. There is a plethora of passages in the Bible that describe Jesus so beautifully, and I do not have the space in this book to look at all of them. But I will look at three that have been particularly meaningful to me, and I pray I will be able to speak of Him in a way that will also touch your hearts.

## A Bruised Reed He Will Not Break

My favorite description of Jesus is in Matthew 12. Matthew is quoting from the prophet Isaiah, and he says: "Here is my servant whom I have chosen, the one I love, in whom I delight; I will put my Spirit on him, and he will proclaim justice to the nations. He will not quarrel or cry out; no one will hear his voice in the streets. A bruised reed he will not break, and a smoldering wick he will not snuff out, till he leads justice to victory. In his name the nations put their hope" (Matthew 12:18-21).

It is fairly obvious that the world is not a kind place. Here in the US we are a divided nation, and everyone seems so angry. The Western world has championed the value of tolerance, but in my lifetime people have only become less tolerant, angrier, and more openly hostile. Social media certainly hasn't helped the kindness factor in our world. It used to be that if you wanted to say something unkind to someone, you had to say it to their face, and it was more likely that you would measure your words when speaking directly to them. But now people write whatever they want on social media and do irreparable damage to relationships with their reckless words. They don't see the person's reaction, nor do they feel the hurtful impact of their words, so they write without regard to the damage being done. We feel entitled to our opinions, and honor is lost in the elevation of our right to express our opinions. But you see, right or left, follower of Jesus or not, it is not kind, and for those who claim to follow Jesus, it doesn't represent Him well.

I think it's important to note that Jesus was gentle with people because He was keenly aware of His Father's love for Him. Matthew notes that He was chosen, loved, and delighted in. If we are going to treat others with dignity and respect, honor and kindness, gentleness and authentic love, we must know that we are deeply loved. We treat others in accordance with the way we truly see ourselves. If we know that we are deeply loved, we can love even those who act in unlovely ways toward us. If we have a keen sense of self-acceptance, we can accept others when they differ from us. And that is what Jesus is like in all His remarkable beauty.

One reason I think it is so important that we get outside the judgments of others, and even ourselves, and see ourselves through the love of Christ, is because only deeply loved people will truly love and accept others. We cannot give what we do not possess. We cannot offer acceptance to others when we do not accept ourselves. What do we mean by tolerance in our society? Our working definition seems to be this: everyone has a right to their opinion, and everyone's opinion is equally valid. Therefore, it is intolerant to disagree with anyone's opinion of themselves or their self-definition. But this isn't really tolerance. This essentially means that a terrorist's opinions are equally valid with the opinions of Mister Rogers. And that is not true.

Our working definition of *tolerance* in the West is designed to undergird the value of diversity, and the latter, I agree, is a noble thing. However, if agreement is necessary for acceptance, then diversity is nothing more than a myth. Our current working approach to tolerance is not working and has led to greater rifts, divisions, and anger. True tolerance means that we will allow people to express their opinions, and we will treat them with dignity and respect. Not that we will agree with them, but we will honor them. Unless we get to the place where we know that we are truly loved and accepted, we will not be accepting, gentle, and kind with those who disagree with us because we must validate ourselves in every interaction. Both sides must be allowed to express their viewpoints, and both sides must treat each other with respect—that is true tolerance.

We judge others through our unprocessed wounds. If we authentically encounter the love of Christ, our wounds will be healed. When our wounds are healed, we will be less judgmental of others. Darcy, part of the answer to your question about why you struggle with the faith of many Christians is because you have run into Christians who are judging others through their woundedness. Too often in the church we substitute learned behavior for authentic encounter that transforms. We settle for knowing the right answers without experiencing the life-changing presence of the risen Christ. Knowledge won't change your heart; *encounter* will.

Jesus found His validation in His Father's unwavering, eternal opinion of Him. All other opinions of Him which were invalidating were merely temporal opinions and therefore held no sway over

> When our relationship with Jesus doesn't make us more loving, there is clearly something wrong with our faith.

Him. He was rooted in the Father's love and, because He knew He was loved and secure, He was able to love everyone, even His enemies. In my own journey, I can assure you, the more I experience God's love, the more I display love to those who disagree with me. When our relationship with Jesus doesn't make us more loving, there is clearly something wrong with our faith. Even if we have no faith, if our way of thinking and living doesn't make us more loving, there is something wrong with our humanity.

I love the Matthew 12 description of Jesus because of the beautiful completeness it displays. Jesus isn't quarrelsome; He isn't a raging, angry man. Far from it: "a bruised reed he will not break, and a smoldering wick he will not snuff out." Feel the tenderness of Jesus in that description. A reed is not like an oak tree, strong and deeply rooted; a reed is pliable and vulnerable. But this reed is also bruised, making it even weaker. Yet Jesus deals with the wounded with extreme tenderness and care. And in the end, we are all wounded people. Some of us have had an easier life than others, but no one lives life without being wounded. Truthfully, my dear children, your life has been better than most. Mom and I are certainly not perfect, but you grew up in a home with stability and love, and that goes a long way to helping someone become rooted in life.

I don't think I understood how good my home life was growing up until I went away to college. I listened to many of my friends talk about their homes, and I realized I was fortunate, more fortunate than most. I remember calling Grandma and Grandpa to tell them that I loved them, and I was grateful. You have been exposed to the painful realities of our world, and you have heard the stories of many who grew up in horribly abusive situations. We have been fortunate, and yet we are not unaffected by this world; we are all still wounded people. No one grows up on this planet without pain, hurt, and hardship. Jesus is tender with all of our wounding.

The passage has more to say: "a smoldering wick He will not snuff out." Again, the description isn't of a roaring fire, but instead a candle whose flame is in danger of going out; a slight breeze could extinguish this flame forever. Jesus sees when our fire is smoldering due to the trials of life; He takes note, He sees, He cares. That's why Jesus came. Everyone has times when their flame flickers in life. Like you, I have experienced the pain of rejection, heartache, and unrequited love. I have felt lost, distant, and far from God and others. I have experienced bouts with discouragement, disappointment, and dark nights of the soul. I was not always aware of the tenderness of Jesus in the darkest hours, but I can now look back on those hours and see He was there, ever so gently coaxing me along. In hindsight, I can see His hand at work, His presence with me, and His redeeming love shaping my soul.

When I took Danielle to school for the first time, I came home, sat in the living room, and wept. Mom sat there with me and wept too, but after a little while she stopped weeping and went on with what she had to do. She came back a while later and I was still weeping. She said, "What's wrong with you?" It wasn't a judgmental statement; she just didn't understand why I was so deeply affected. Part of it was my own wounding; I had separation anxiety growing up, and going to school was emotionally trying for me. Jesus, in His tenderness, met me later in life and healed that separation anxiety, allowing me to do what I do now and travel around the world without angst. But part of the reason I wept was because I knew I could no longer protect you and that you would be impacted and hurt by this broken world we live in. I wept tears of grief for all the pain you would experience in life—and not just for Danielle. I wept that day for each of you since Danielle represented the first of you to head to school. That day I wept the tears of the tenderness of Jesus, for as His tenderness has met me, I have cried more tears for the pain of others.

But you see, the beauty of the passage is not just in Jesus' gentle love, it's in His passion for justice: "a bruised reed he will not break, and a smoldering wick he will not snuff out, till he leads justice to victory." He isn't just a kind and caring Savior who overlooks the wrongs in the world. He cares for the oppressed, and one day He will eliminate all oppression. He isn't weak or unable to contend with evil. He is patient, giving all of us countless opportunities to correct our wayward ways, but He is not weak or indifferent to pain. The Apostle John describes Heaven with these words: "God's dwelling place is now among the people, and he will dwell with them. They will be his people, and God himself will be with them and be their God. He will wipe every tear from their eyes. There will be no more death or mourning or crying or pain, for the old order of things has passed away" (Revelation 21:3, 4). He is creating everything new, and evil will be done away with, injustice eliminated, and pure, unadulterated goodness and love reign without interruption. He will lead justice to victory. One day, sin, evil, oppression, and death will be ushered out the door.

In the meantime, Jesus has left the assignment to His followers to advance the Kingdom of light in the midst of the darkness. We are to represent His kindness and passion for justice. We are to right wrongs and care for outcasts. We are to address injustice and do good in this evil world. In Jesus' name we are to be His hands and feet and represent Him well to those who do not know His tender love. And if you look at the history of the church, much good has been done in His name: hospitals, literacy programs, and countless charitable organizations that seek to bring help and healing to humanity have been established by Christ's followers. Sadly, however, as we talked about in the Introduction, the followers of Jesus have not always represented Him well. That doesn't make these things less true about Jesus; it makes these things less true about us. That's why Jesus came. We need Him.

I once went through a season in which I was betrayed by some people who were close to me. I had forgiven those who hurt me, and I thought I had come through the other side, but one day I was out for a bike ride and tears were streaming down my face as I rode. I said, "Lord, what is that?" I sensed Jesus saying to me, "I'm pulling grief out of you." I went home and sat in the living room with Jesus. I could sense His tenderness, I could feel the pain of the betrayals, and tears streamed down my face. For a few months I experienced this fairly regularly until the tenderness of Jesus had healed my wounds and my tears dried up. This is the Jesus I know and love.

## Our High Priest

That leads me to the second passage I want to highlight. It isn't difficult for any honest person to see that the world has been tainted by evil, or what the Bible calls sin. But it isn't just a problem with the world; sadly, it is a personal problem. You remember the time when Danielle was little and cut her own hair? She got a pair of scissors and cut off a hunk of her hair—and it was not a neat and tidy haircut! She was standing on the stairs and Mom saw her with a massive gap in her hairline. In one hand she held the offending scissors, and in the other she held the missing hunk of hair. Mom exclaimed in horror, "Danielle! You cut your hair!" To which Danielle immediately replied, "No I didn't." That answer wasn't convincing.

No one ever had to teach any of us to hide or lie. All it ultimately means to be a sinner is that we have an innate desire to go our own way, to do our own thing; we have an undeniable bias toward self. We tend to make life too much about ourselves, and when we are caught in wrongdoing, we cover up and hide. It's human nature. From God's perspective sin had to be addressed, and that is why Jesus came to earth. We needed a Savior—someone who could represent us before God and offer us forgiveness, a new start in life, and the power to change.

When I was a kid, Uncle Ken and I played a lot of sports with the other kids in the neighborhood. This wasn't organized sports with adult supervision; it was kids managing their own game with their own rules. We probably spent half our time arguing whether a ball was fair or foul, or whether that was pass interference or a legal defensive play. And often when an argument was going nowhere, we simply called a "do-over." We would end the argument and just do the play again. The problem with life is you don't get do-overs; you can't undo marital unfaithfulness or take back damaging, angry words. But you can be forgiven . . . over and over again, and with the help of God, you can change. The tenderness of Jesus extends to all our weakness and sin.

Sometimes the church has gotten hung up on certain sins—sexual sin, for example, has gotten a lot of attention through the years. But the problem isn't with how you sin, the problem is that we are all sinners. Being a sinner just means we do things that are wrong, hurtful to others, and selfish. We want to define our own way of right and wrong, and we don't want anyone else to tell us otherwise. We push God out of the center and go our own way. That's what it means to be a sinner. I never get hung up on any particular type of sin. You have all made decisions that are wrong, and so have I, but it doesn't bother me, nor do I have any judgment for you because you sin. It saddens me sometimes, but the thing I long for is that you would put Jesus at the center of your lives, because He is worthy and life works better when we follow Jesus. He loves us whether we follow Him or not, but there is enormous advantage to going God's way. This is what I have discovered. I, too, as you know better than most, am a sinner, and I have done many things that are wrong.

I don't live life with shame because of Jesus' grace to me, but I do have a lot of regrets. If I could live life over, I would do many things different. Sometimes I ask people, "If you could do life over, what would you do differently?" Sadly, the most common answer I receive is, "Nothing." I think to myself: Wow! You didn't learn a thing. Or: you are making life way too much about you—what about all the people you hurt with your actions? Wouldn't you change some things, if you could do them again, for their sake? I would. I would do lots of things over—I would be a better father, a better husband, a better follower of Jesus. I would love people more tenderly and display more patience and kindness. I would be more attentive and less preoccupied. I don't get to do life over, but I do get to access Jesus' forgiveness over and over again.

From the writer of Hebrews: "Therefore, since we have a great high priest who ascended into heaven, Jesus the Son of

> I don't get to do life over, but I do get to access Jesus' forgiveness over and over again.

God, let us hold firmly to the faith we profess. For we do not have a high priest who is unable to empathize with our weakness, but we have one who has been tempted in every way, just as we are—yet he did not sin. Let us then approach God's throne of grace with confidence so that we may receive mercy and find grace to help us in our time of need" (Hebrews 4:14-16).

Jesus is the perfect bridge between Heaven's perfection and earth's fallenness. He is God's eternal Son, and He left Heaven to become one of us. He entered our sin-stricken, evil-ridden world, and He endured temptation and evil like the rest of us. He suffered loss—His earthly father likely died when He was young. He was betrayed by some of His closest friends. He was tempted with sin just like us, but He overcame temptation. He was misunderstood, mistreated, and persecuted. He was oppressed and falsely accused by religious people and political leaders.

The fact that He knows what life is like on a broken planet means He has true compassion for our failings, heartaches, and pain. When sin entered the world, God could have left the mess we created to us, alone, to figure out. But He didn't. He intervened in a spectacular way—by becoming one of us and subjecting Himself to the mess we humans created. Jesus entered into our suffering; He suffered with us, and He suffered for us on the cross. The reality is there are a lot of things in this world I do not understand. I don't understand why God intervenes sometimes and miraculously heals one person with cancer, and yet another person dies. I have preached on healing and had people line up for prayer, and I have prayed for sick people and seen one person in line miraculously healed and the person right after them not. I don't understand why things happen the way they do, but I know God cares because Jesus came and suffered with us and for us. He didn't come to judge us or condemn us, He came to save us. He came to offer forgiveness and hope, assurance that God cares and that this world is not the final chapter.

Do you remember the time I was on a mission trip to Ecuador, and I got as sick as I have ever been? While I was sick, I prayed for a woman in a wheelchair, and she was miraculously healed. She stood up, walked to the podium, and testified that Jesus heals. It was powerful. Later that night I was walking on top of the mountain in Quito, and I was talking with my pastor, friend, and translator, Renato, about the miracle we had seen that morning. I said to him, "I have never actually experienced healing myself, even though I have seen some pretty cool miracles in my lifetime." Just after I said that I sensed the Lord say to me: *Do you want to be healed?* I said, "Yes!" He said, *Lay your hand on your stomach.* As soon as I did, I instantly felt better. I hadn't eaten in five days, but we went out for dinner that night, and I ate barbecue! Why did God wait five days to ask me if I wanted healing? I don't know. People had been praying for me, but I wasn't healed for five days. Why was I healed then? I honestly don't know, but I was grateful!

Yet Craig has diabetes and we have prayed and fasted for him to be healed, we had other people pray that he would be healed, and God has not healed him. Why? I don't know. But I know Jesus is the man of sorrows, acquainted with suffering, as the Scripture says. I know He cares for us in all our pain, and I know Heaven will be a place untainted by sin and evil and all its effects. In Heaven, Craig will not have diabetes!

In the meantime, be sure of this: Jesus empathizes with your hurts, trials, tribulations, hardships, sin, and failings. He knows you and loves you at your very best, and He understands you and loves you at your very worst. He is present with empathetic understanding and tenderness to help you through life's most troubling times. The invitation for you and me is to approach the throne of Heaven, where Jesus sits victorious over evil, sin, and death, and to be assured that He will plead our case before the Father because He is our High Priest.

In Jewish circles, the high priest would go into the temple and offer a sacrifice for the sins of the people. He represented the people to God and God to the people. He interceded on the people's behalf; he was a mediator between God and humanity. The high priest, however, was a flawed human just like the rest of us, and he not only offered God's forgiveness to the people, he also needed forgiveness himself. But Jesus is no ordinary high priest. He was tempted but did not sin. He didn't just offer a sacrifice or petition on our behalf; He offered His life as our sacrifice on the cross in exchange for our new life in Him. Paul writes, "God made him who had no sin to be sin for us, so that in him we might become the righteousness of God" (2 Corinthians 5:21). He became sin; we became accepted. He became dirty with our wrongs so we could become clean with His rights. This is the beautiful tenderness of Jesus on our behalf.

It isn't just that Jesus wiped out our moral debts before God. He deposited His perfect holiness into our eternal bank account. In banking terms, we had an insurmountable debt, and Jesus didn't only wipe out the debt and give us a zero balance. Jesus wiped out our debt and deposited His riches in our account. We went from bankrupt to rich like royalty in a dramatic, divine shift. All it takes to receive this gift is humility. We have to humble ourselves and receive the gift God has provided us in Christ. Then we can approach the Father like Jesus the Son. If we understood, if we truly experienced, how much God loves us, it would radically change the way we interact with Him and others. We would pray with more confidence. We would love with less judgment because we are loved. We would walk in more honest humility because of the security we have in God's love.

When you come to God, you can approach the throne of grace. Notice it is not a throne of judgment. God has more grace than you have sin; God has more acceptance than you have shame. God has more mercy than you have wrongs. This is why we can come to God through Jesus no matter what evil thing we have done, no matter how entrenched we are in a broken place or in a destructive pattern of behavior. With Jesus you never need to hide or pretend or cover up. No matter what you have done, no matter what you are doing, you are welcome to come to the Father for help because of Jesus our High Priest. Jesus cares, He understands, and He has compassion for you. The mistake we make is always in hiding, rather than humbling ourselves and coming honestly. Jesus is irresistibly attracted to the contrite of heart. He never refuses a needy sinner who comes in humility.

Jesus calls us to repent, which means He invites us to get into proper alignment with God. This is because life works better for us when we are in right alignment with God. You remember when Darcy was little, how she used to wander?

We lived on Route 18, a busy street, and when she was not yet four years old she went outside and started to cross the street to leave a note for our neighbors, the Stoehrs. The police saw her and brought her to our door. Mom and I, along with the police, didn't want her to cross the street—not because we are mean, but because we didn't want her to get hurt. So they brought her back to the safety of our home. Repentance is returning to the safety of God's house. This is why God calls us to follow Him, and when we wander, He calls us to repent. He is calling us back home, into His presence. It isn't with judgment that He calls us home; it is with the tender heart of love.

I have listened to the stories of people who have experienced the worst of things. They have been victims of violence, sexual abuse, rape, torture, torment, and hideous human behaviors. When I listen to their stories, my heart is deeply moved with the tenderness Jesus feels for them. But I have also listened to people confess every imaginable evil deed: murder, rape, adultery, acts of violence, pedophilia, incest, sexual abuse, and every other horrible thing humans do to one another. Yet when I see that any person who has committed such an act is truly contrite, I find myself feeling compassion for them. It is the supernatural tenderness of Jesus that rises up for sinners authentically repentant for their sin. I can sense Jesus welcoming them home. There is always room for us to come home to God, no matter what, because Jesus is our High Priest.

## The Light of the World

The Apostle John had a unique relationship with Jesus. Part of that was probably because he was so young; he was likely only a teenager when he started following Jesus. He often refers to himself as "the one Jesus loved." Of course, Jesus loved all the disciples, but John internalized Christ's love and personalized it in a way that carried him through life with confident strength. In the prologue to his Gospel, John writes the third description of Jesus that I want to explore.

John writes, "In the beginning was the Word, and the Word was with God, and the Word was God. He was with God in the beginning. Through him all things were made; without him nothing was made that has been made. In him was life, and that life was the light of all people. The light shines in the darkness, and the darkness has not overcome it" (John 1:1-5).

Jesus spoke the world into existence in the beginning. One of the things I know about being a father is that it makes you love someone irrationally. There is no reason why I loved the four of you more than I loved other children. You were good children, but let's be honest, you might not be the best children in the world! I know it is hard to believe, but there have been others who were smarter, and others who were better looking or perhaps better behaved at times. But even if another child was better looking, better behaved, or did better in school, they were never going to compete with my affections for you. There is no reason for that other than the fact that you are my children. God made you for me, and that established a deep love inside of me that will not be broken. You have made, and will make, choices in life that I would not want you to make, but that will never end my love for you. You may not love me in return, but I will go on loving you. The only thing that can prevent a father or mother from loving their child is their own sinfulness, not the child's misdeeds. The parent gets hurt, disappointed, upset, angry, and does not process that well, so they harden their heart to love so they will not be hurt anymore. But I will not do that.

And God cannot do that, because God is love, as John tells us in his first epistle (1 John 4:16). God's love for us, in that sense, is irrational. It isn't deserved; it isn't earned. God doesn't love us because of who we are or what we do or what we have, God loves us because of who He is. He created us because He is love, and He continues to love us because He continues to be love. Sin did not, and cannot, disrupt the love of God. That's why Jesus came. Your acceptance or rejection of God will not cause God to love you more or love you less. All our rejection will do is cause us to miss out on the greatest love this world has ever known.

Unfortunately, what sin did was create barriers between us and God and us and other people. Jesus came as the light of the world to show us what God is like. When Jesus shines light into our hearts to show us something is out of alignment with God, He never shines light to make us feel bad. Jesus shines light to get us free. He shines light to bring us back into alignment with God, because He loves us and wants our best. The light that Jesus shines into our lives doesn't change reality; light merely reveals what is true. If we were in a pitch-black room full of all sorts of things, when someone turned on the light, it would not change what was in the room, it would merely reveal what was there. God shines light to help us, but so often we feel some degree of shame over what we have done, and we do not want to stand in the light with God and others. We feel defensive and want to justify ourselves, and we refuse to humble ourselves before God and receive His loving acceptance. We miss the opportunity the light affords.

When I buy a new car, I read the manual to see how to best care for that car, because I assume the creator of the car knows best how the car operates optimally. In the same way, the Bible teaches us that God loves us most and knows what's best for us. Jesus didn't come to condemn or shame or judge, so when He shines light into our lives it isn't to make us feel guilty. He simply does it out of love and longing for our best and for the best of others.

> God shines light to help us, but so often we feel some degree of shame over what we have done, and we do not want to stand in the light with God and others.

But as you might expect, people don't always receive truth well, even if it is given with the best of intentions. The light Jesus offered was not well received, but John tells us that the darkness could not overcome it. Light always dispels darkness; darkness cannot overcome light. Sadly, John goes on to say, "He was in the world, and though the world was made through him, the world did not recognize him. He came to that which was his own, but his own did not receive him" (John 1:10, 11).

One of the great mysteries of life is the vulnerability of Jesus. Jesus was with God, and Jesus was God, yet He made himself a human and opened Himself up to rejection. And He did receive rejection and has been receiving it ever since. He was rejected, yet He did not become angry, hardened, or embittered because of His supremely loving nature and selfless intentions. The tenderness of Jesus is on display every time a sinner rejects His invitation to relationship.

Anytime anyone is willing to receive Him, He always accepts them. "Yet to all who did receive him, to those who believed in his name, he gave the right to become children of God—children born not of natural descent, nor of human decision or a husband's will, but born of God" (John 1:12, 13). Jesus came to create a path back to God for anyone who was willing. He won't force anyone; that is what oppressors and abusers do. He simply loves, woos, waits, and invites. He reveals His love to us and welcomes us to receive it. The tenderness of Jesus is always revealed through the rejection He experiences. To be rejected and to love in return, that is the most sincerely beautiful love I know.

Jesus longs for every man to be His brother and every woman to be His sister. He longs for all of us to be in His family. In this world of isolation and loneliness, Jesus is the gateway to belonging in the family of God. Just as we must be born physically to join a human family, we must be born spiritually to join God's family. You were born into this world because Mom and I chose to have children of our own, and that is the only way you could enter our family, through parental choice. To enter God's family, though, requires a mutual choice. God chose to pave the way through Jesus for all to enter; now we must choose Him. We must say "yes" to what He has done for us. The more we are convinced of His compassionate love, the more we long to belong to and behave like the family of God.

After we choose faith in Jesus for forgiveness and salvation, we must choose to follow Jesus. That is Jesus' call in our lives. He bids us to come into relationship, to do life together, but not as equals—He is Lord of all. He is the King of Heaven, and regardless of human choice, Heaven's King He will remain. He wants us to put Him at the center of our lives, to factor Him into all our choices and decisions. Jesus calls us to come and follow Him. After the relationship breakup early in my life that I referred to earlier, I chose to make Jesus the center of my life. I have surely failed and sinned often since that day, but I can sincerely say that I have made it my life's intention to make Jesus the center of all I do. Following Jesus has made my life better; I have never regretted following Him. All my regrets in life come back to those ways in which I have not followed Him as closely or represented Him as well as I could have.

John goes on to write, "The Word became flesh and made his dwelling among us. We have seen his glory, the glory of the one and only Son, who came from the Father, full of grace and truth" (John 1:14). I love this description of Jesus. He made His dwelling among us. He set up His home in the middle of our troubled world. He popped his tent in our human villages troubled by sin and dysfunction. He didn't have to, but love compelled Him to do so. While He was here, He revealed His glory to us. Jesus displayed His glory through His miracles, through His victories over temptation, through His exorcisms of demonic beings to set people free, through His power over the laws of nature, and perhaps most of all, through His tenderness. Throughout His time here on our globe He displayed tenderness to the rich and the poor, the Jew and the Gentile, the healthy and the sick, the righteous and the sinful, to those who received Him and those who rejected Him. Jesus displayed the tenderness of the Father's heart to all of us so we would know what God is truly like. This is the Jesus I know and love; this is why I have been so inspired to follow wholeheartedly after Him.

This past year Mom let the grass grow long in a "no mow May" campaign. As a result we had a field in our side yard, and we ended up with two families of baby bunnies in that portion of the yard. We didn't know they were there at first, and when I cut the lawn, they were sadly exposed. Their nest was still intact, but no longer protected by the high grasses. Of course, if I had known they were there, I would have allowed the grass to grow unhindered until they had grown up, because I love animals. But I didn't know, and sadly the world is a cruel place for vulnerable little creatures. One family of bunnies got diseases and all the babies died. Courtney and I did our best to help them, but they were too sick. The other family of baby bunnies appeared to be doing well, but they were in the open . . . and Muffin the cat discovered them. We kept him inside, because every time we let him outside, he made a beeline straight for the bunnies. I felt compassion for the vulnerable baby bunnies, but I also felt compassion for Muffin, the murderous cat. I felt bad that this creature was trapped inside when we all know how much Muffin loves to be out. So I started letting Muffin out, but with supervision! I would stand guard over the bunnies' nest, like a centurion, keeping the evil cat from killing the defenseless bunnies.

As I sat there guarding the vulnerable creatures and having compassion for the cooped-up cat, I thought about the heart of God. The world is a harsh, cruel place for the weak, the young, the vulnerable, and the oppressed. Jesus came for the wounded, the hurting, and the oppressed. In His marvelous tenderness He came for the afflicted to let them know He cares, He heals, and that He is here with you and for you. Jesus is tender with you when you feel hurt, rejected, wounded, anxious, nervous, fearful, and depressed. He loves you when life beats you down. He loves you when you seek to follow Him, but stumble and fall, and He loves you when you stop following Him and live in open opposition to His desires. He is for you, not against you.

But He also came for the oppressors: to shine light, to offer a better path, to call them to repent, and to have mercy on those who would accept His invitation to repent. To forgive those who turn away from sin and follow Him. All of us at one point or another have been the wounded and the wounder, the hurt and the hurter; we have been those sinned against and those sinning against others. Jesus loves you when you are the one wounded by the sin of another, and Jesus loves you when you are the one wounding others by your sin. He loves you whether you are a baby bunny or a murderous house cat that longs to be outside. And that is why Jesus came. He came for you in all His tenderness.

When I was a kid I used to play a lot of sports with the other kids in the neighborhood. One time we were in our backyard playing some game, and I swore. That wasn't unusual. But Grandma heard me; that was unusual. I can't remember if she called me inside then, or if she talked to me later. But I do remember sitting down and talking to her about it. I felt bad because I got caught and Grandma was upset—so there was shame. But in the conversation Grandma said to me that it was hurtful to Jesus when I spoke like that, and that brought tears to my eyes. I didn't change, though. Years later when I had that encounter with Jesus after the breakup, I was moved to change in all sorts of areas of life. I saw Jesus standing in front of me waiting to embrace me, but I was rejecting Him, and then something inside me shifted. I experienced the vulnerability of Jesus—that He opened Himself to be rejected by those He had come for—and I experienced the tenderness of Jesus. I realized He wasn't angry with me, He just wanted to be close to me, but I had refused. It was so moving that I decided that day I would follow Jesus wholeheartedly. I have been seeking to follow Him wholeheartedly since. That is the power of encountering Jesus' tender love.

Dear children, I often pray that you would know Jesus as He is, not as you have seen Him misrepresented by others. It is my deepest desire that you would encounter Him for yourselves, not merely know about Him. There is no one else like Jesus. He is the most beautiful, the most compelling, the most inspiring person I know. He has completely captured my heart's affections because I have met Him and experienced Him. This is what I long for, that all of you would experience this in ever-deepening realities. No one else can heal your soul, salve your wounds, revive your heart, cleanse your sins, release you from guilt, break your shame, and fill you with acceptance.

### Experience

Sit with Jesus for a moment. Picture Him sitting with you in your house or car or wherever you are. Tell Him what is on your heart: the hurts, the offenses, the pain, the heartache, the mistakes, the guilt, the sin, the shame. Think about these images of Jesus: *A bruised reed He will not break, a smoldering wick He will not snuff out.* He is your *High Priest* who understands. He is the *light* who has come into the world, full of truth and full of grace. After presenting to Jesus what is on your heart, wait for Him to minister His tender love to you, speak to you, and give you needed help.

*"Every day we may see some new thing in Christ.*
*His love hath neither brim nor bottom."*
— Samuel Rutherford

Two
———

# TENDER ACTS

When you read through the Gospels with eyes to see and ears to hear, you discover Jesus' tender actions on nearly every page. As I set out to write this chapter for you, I culled through all four Gospels looking at potential stories to consider, and I had more than two dozen stories from which to choose. I could write multiple books just examining Jesus' tender interactions with people through the four Gospels, but for the sake of keeping this book short, I will only look at three stories, one from each of the synoptic Gospels (Matthew, Mark, and Luke; we will look at something from John's Gospel later). The three stories I'll examine here show the breadth and depth of Jesus' compassion. In these stories we find Jesus interacting with men, women, foreigners, crowds, sick people, demonized people, and his closest friends.

## A Desperate Mom

A desperate woman approached Jesus one day on behalf of her daughter who was being tormented by a demonic spirit (Matthew 15:21-28). The woman is described as a "Canaanite"; the Canaanites were enemies of the Israelites in the Old Testament. They worshipped other deities and did not follow Yahweh, yet somehow this woman has heard of Jesus, and she believes Jesus can help her daughter. He has slipped out of Israel and into the region of Tyre and Sidon, most likely to withdraw from the crowds and allow Himself a break. Jesus often used geography to get away from people and take a retreat for self-restoration. He frequently used mountains, deserts, boats on water, deserted places, and even surrounding foreign lands to get away from the constantly present and relentlessly pressing crowds. But it was hard for Him to get away, and in this story, once again He is discovered.

The woman cries out, "Lord, Son of David, have mercy on me! My daughter is demon-possessed and suffering terribly" (Matthew 15:22). First, I want you to notice the way the woman addresses Jesus. The titles she uses—Lord, and Son of David—were Israelite titles for the Messiah; they are titles of reverence and clearly demonstrate faith. This from a Canaanite woman! Second, let me briefly talk about the subject of demons. Many modern commentators assume the woman's daughter is mentally ill and that first-century people attributed what we would call mental illness to demons. However, I would argue that many people in the Western world simply do not have eyes to see or ears to hear (as Jesus often says). Our Western worldview has blinded us to the spiritual realities that Jesus understood. You cannot take the Gospels or Jesus seriously without understanding that there are dark, spiritual entities that torment people. The Gospel accounts are littered with stories of Jesus delivering people from demons that created all sorts of symptoms. Jesus was not a country bumpkin who couldn't discern between a psychological issue and a demonic issue. He did deliverance because people had demons and needed deliverance. Personally, I do not like the translation "demon-possessed" because it implies ownership, but the Greek word doesn't. I think we should just call it "demonization," which is a transliteration of the Greek word.

One last thing: I have, as you know, done thousands of deliverances on people, and they have been freed from all sorts of maladies like anxiety, depression, certain temptations, nightmares, and a host of other things. They had been to church, been through discipleship, therapy—and nothing helped. Immediately after their deliverance, they were free. I was recently in Australia and a woman approached me and said, "You were here in 2017. I had experienced anxiety and panic attacks every week for the previous thirteen years. After the deliverance session I have never experienced anxiety or panic attacks again." For this woman, it has been six years without any symptoms. I could tell you thousands of stories like that. You can't cast out "human," but you can't educate, medicate, or counsel demons. When a person has a demonic issue, the only solution for relief is deliverance. Jesus understood this.

I suppose a lot of other people would not have chosen this passage to describe the tenderness of Jesus because of Jesus' initial response to the woman's appeal. He is silent. "Jesus did not answer a word" (Matthew 15:23). That is an odd response and, if you read the rest of the Gospel accounts, you will discover that this is not typical of Jesus. Why does He remain silent when the woman is so deeply distressed? I know you may be tempted to look at this response and assume Jesus is uncaring, indifferent, or even hard-hearted. But I think His atypical response should give us pause. Whenever Jesus does something that is out of character for Him, it should make you ponder why. I think there are a few possibilities.

First, Jesus is likely tired and spending time in this Gentile region for the very purpose of getting a break. As I said above, this is one of His retreat strategies. Jesus was fully human, and He got tired, hungry, thirsty, and sleepy just like you. He had emotional and spiritual limitations when He walked upon the earth, just like all of us. So Jesus needed to take a break and re-plenish from time to time. Imagine how busy and in-demand Jesus was because of all the miracles He did and the wisdom with which He spoke. But I don't think this is the reason he didn't, at first, speak.

Second, Jesus may have been silent because of the disci-ples. He may have been trying to teach them something. They came to Jesus because the woman was relentlessly crying out, and they said, "Send her away, for she keeps crying out af-ter us" (Matthew 15:23). The word used here for "send her away" is the word often used by Matthew either for divorce or dismissing a crowd that has gathered when it is time for them to go home. The word is vague enough that they could have meant, "Send her away after you heal her daughter." But that seems unlikely. They too are tired, and she is relentless, crying out. And she is a foreigner—a Canaanite "dog" (this was a common Jewish insult for the Canaanites due to their long-standing enmity). In short, it is likely that the disciples were prejudiced, and Jesus needed to address it somehow, be-cause Jesus came to lead justice to victory.

Jesus responds to the disciples' request to send her away by saying, "I was sent only to the lost sheep of Israel" (Matthew 15:24). If the disciples were asking Jesus to send her away after healing the woman's daughter, then Jesus is explaining to them why He is not responding to her cry for help: His Father's assignment was for Him to begin with the Israelites. If the disciples were trying to get Jesus to get rid of her, Jesus is reiterating their Jewish mindset. Let me give you a little bit of history here. The traditional Old Testament understanding of the Messiah was that He was a Jewish Messiah who was coming to deliver the Israelites from the long-standing oppression they had suffered under Gentile nations. In other words: He came for the Jews, not for the Gentiles. The Gentiles were the oppressors, and the Jewish people had a long history of suffering. When you read the Gospels, in fact, Jesus does most of His ministry to the Jewish people because He does begin His ministry with Israel. He seeks to mobilize the Jewish people to be a light to the Gentiles, which was part of God's purpose for them.

You might remember that God chose the Israelites and intended two purposes for His people. First, they would be a holy people. They would be pure, loyal to God, follow God's ways, and avoid the evil practices of the surrounding nations. God was looking for them to be like a loving, loyal bride. In the Old Testament He compares Himself to a husband and Israel to His bride. You might not know this, but the nations around Israel were worshipping demonic beings, engaging in temple prostitution, sacrificing their children in the fire, and participating in a host of other deplorable activities. God wanted His children to avoid these evil things and be a consecrated people, a nation set apart to God's holy ways. But secondly,

He wanted His people to be a light to the Gentiles. He wanted His people to represent Him well to the rest of humanity. He wanted His people to lead the Gentiles to know Him and follow His ways.

However, things didn't work out so well.

The Israelites, rather than separating themselves, engaged in the evil acts of their neighbors. God kept calling them to repent, but they kept rebelling. The Israelites ended up divided in a civil war that resulted in two nations: Judah and Israel. Israel, the Northern kingdom, eventually ended up in captivity (to Assyria) and assimilated into other people groups. The Southern kingdom, Judah, also ended up in captivity (to Babylonia), but eventually was restored to the land. When the Southern kingdom returned, the people had learned their lesson. They gave up idolatry and the evil practices of the neighboring peoples and became separatists. But sadly, this left them with a prejudice against Gentiles (who also often became oppressive to the Jews), and the Hebrew people abandoned their mission to become a light in the darkness. They could not figure out how to be holy and on mission.

This is the historical backdrop of this conversation with the disciples. They are Jewish separatists and truly believe Jesus is strictly a Jewish Messiah. At the end of the Gospel of Matthew, Jesus commands them to take this gospel to all peoples—and this shows you Jesus' heart. One of the things clear about Jesus is that everyone mattered to Him. Peter, in his second epistle, writes that the Lord is not slow in returning, but that He wishes that none should perish (2 Peter 3:9). Jesus compassionately longs for all people to know Him and experience His healing love and forgiveness. And in this story with the Canaanite woman, I think Jesus is starting to break down the disciples' deep-seated prejudice, and this is a hard lesson for them to learn.

In the book of Acts we see that Peter is still struggling to learn this lesson. Jesus gives him a vision to prepare him to go to Cornelius, a Gentile man seeking the truth, and the vision convinces Peter that Gentiles are not "unclean" anymore (Acts 10). Peter stands up and fights for the Gentiles to be included, but even after this he struggles again, and this is revealed in a conversation Paul records for us in Galatians 2. In that case, Peter wouldn't eat with some Gentiles because of the prejudicial pressure from some legalistic Jewish converts. Prejudice is evil, and it is one of the injustices that Jesus wants to break, as He "leads justice to victory."

Sadly, my generation did not always represent the justice of Jesus well. I think that is one of the reasons why so many in your generation have struggled with the goodness of God and the tenderness of Jesus. When I was talking with Darcy on our trip around Maui, I reminded her of the time I preached against racism and had various people of color from our church come up and tell stories about how they had been mistreated. It was a beautiful, moving service, and I am grateful that I did that decades ago. But I also regret I did not do more.

Now let me take you back to the story so you can see the tenderness of Jesus in it.

Jesus remains silent, but the woman keeps after Him for help, and the disciples start pleading with Him to dismiss her. Jesus gives voice to their Jewish mindset: "I was only sent to the lost sheep of Israel." It is also true of His initial assignment from the Father: He was to start His Kingdom mission with the lost sheep of Israel, who would hopefully respond and then fulfill their mission to be a light to the Gentiles. The woman sees this statement from Jesus as a door cracked open, and she kneels before Jesus. You have to understand that the word used here for kneel in the original language is a word used for an act of worship: to bow down before someone as an act of reverence. Matthew clearly sees that this woman has faith in Jesus—by the titles she uses (Lord, Son of David) and the humble act of worship she engages in—and she is declaring her belief in Jesus as a wonder-working Lord.

As she kneels before Jesus with a broken heart for her daughter, she says, "Lord, help me!" Jesus replies, "It is not right to take the children's bread and toss it to the dogs" (Matthew 15:26). I mentioned earlier that the Jews used the derogatory expression "dogs" to describe the Gentiles; the word they used was something akin to "mangy mutt." But Jesus softens it slightly with the woman and uses a word that is used for a household pet. Nonetheless, He is clearly attempting to do two things: first, He is engaging with the woman to tease out her faith; He wants the disciples to see her faith. Second, He is attempting to shift His disciples' thinking.

The woman's response to Jesus' phrase is utterly beautiful: "'Yes it is, Lord,' she said. 'Even the dogs eat the crumbs that fall from their master's table.'" Children, you know what it's like to have pet dogs. When we had Tootsie, we didn't set her a place at the table like one of you four children, but she did get a lot of scraps—and she stole some that no one gave her! This woman is saying to Jesus, "I don't need to be treated like one of the Jewish children, but I would be happy to get some of the Kingdom scraps that fall from your table."

And Jesus gives her the whole meal. He said to her, "Woman, you have great faith! Your request is granted" (Matthew 15:28). There are only two times Jesus describes

He never tests your faith so you will fail; He only tests your faith to coax it out into deeper waters where intimacy is cultivated, where the power of God is released.

someone as having "great faith" in the Gospels, and significantly, both times it is a Gentile that He commends: the Syrophoenician woman here, and the Roman centurion (Matthew 10:10). Jesus knew that great faith was within her, and His actions were choreographed to bring it out, to display it, for all to see. His celebration of her great faith revealed that He was rooting for her all along, just as He always roots for you. He never tests your faith so you will fail; He only tests your faith to coax it out into deeper waters where intimacy is cultivated, where the power of God is released.

Jesus is also communicating to the disciples that Gentiles can have authentic faith and belong to the family of God. There are no inferior people, no dogs, no one who is disqualified in God's Kingdom. What qualifies someone for God's favorable response is humble faith, not the color of their skin, their nationality, their birth order, their economic status, or their educational background. You can have nothing but faith and receive everything you need from God. No one who comes with faith is found "unclean" in God's Kingdom.

I know that sometimes the people of God have not always represented Jesus' tender heart well—to you and the world around us. I know that on my very best day I am merely a poor reflection of Jesus' magnanimity. And if you're honest, you will have to admit that you are not flawlessly representing the tender heart of Jesus to those around you either. But none of these failings take away from who Jesus really is. I want you to know the beautiful tenderness that this woman held on for and experienced.

You see, this story is in the Bible to teach us, too. It teaches us that the tender heart of Jesus has room for everyone: Jew and Gentile, male and female, oppressed and repentant oppressor. It reveals to us that the tenderness of Jesus is available today. We too must come with a faith that holds on, trusting in the unrelenting largeness of Jesus' compassion. Jesus is seeking to coax you and I out into the deeper waters of faith where we can receive the fullness of His favor. Years ago I decided that I would not take offense at God anymore; I found that often in times of testing, I took offense at God. I interpreted the silence of Jesus as personal rejection, and I was hurt by the perceived slight. But I was distancing myself from Him and unintentionally hardening my heart, and I knew I needed to choose a new path. Jesus has proven His tenderness to me—most importantly on the cross, but also through my own history with God. He has redeemed pain in my life in so many ways through hardship in marriage, parenting, finances, and ministry. I have experienced the tenderness of Jesus over and over through the most difficult times in life. Pain subsides, and life will end, but the tenderness of Jesus will last forever. Hold on to that. This is why I covenanted with God to never take offense at Him again. It forces me to process all my hurt and disappointment and keep my heart open to God. It has made a world of difference.

> Pain subsides, and life will end, but the tenderness of Jesus will last forever. Hold on to that.

There are many times when a child wants something that is not best for them, and our parental heartstrings pull on us with tenderness as a parent. We want to make life easier and more comfortable for them. But if we always give the child everything they want and demonstrate no strength to make tough choices, we will ultimately hurt them. If we remove them from all pain and trial, our children will grow up to be weak and codependent. Jesus isn't like that. He had great tenderness for this woman, for her daughter, and for the disciples. He had to figure out how to act in tenderness and fortify her strength and break down the fortress of the disciples' prejudice. He kept the smoldering wick burning while continuing to lead justice to victory. That's who Jesus is.

## Tired and Hungry People

Jesus sends His disciples out to preach the Gospel of the Kingdom and heal the sick and cast out demons (Mark 6:6-13). After they return from a successful ministry trip, they come back to tell Jesus everything that happened. Sadly, they also discover that John the Baptist has been killed (Mark 6:14-29). They had just spent a lot of spiritual energy in ministry and emotional energy through grief, and Jesus knows that they need to replenish. "The apostles gathered around Jesus and reported to him all they had done and taught. Then, because so many people were coming and going that they did not even have a chance to eat, he said to them, 'Come with me by yourselves to a quiet place and get some rest'" (Mark 6:30, 31).

In this story Jesus' tenderness comes through to me in multiple ways. First, as I mentioned earlier, I always see and feel

Jesus' tenderness through His vulnerability. He didn't have to subject Himself to suffering, but He did. In the opening scene of this story of the feeding of the multitude, Jesus is experiencing grief over the death of a loved one, His cousin and forerunner, John the Baptist, who had been beheaded. John is the first who professes who Jesus is: "Look, the Lamb of God, who takes away the sin of the world!" (John 1:29). John is the one who starts preaching on the Kingdom, he prepares the way for Jesus, and he encourages his own followers to follow Jesus because that is why he has come: to point people to Jesus. He is a selfless, loyal comrade, and now John dies a cruel, brutal, unjust death. Jesus is moved with grief. Matthew tells us in his preamble to the feeding of the five thousand that after Jesus heard about John's death "he withdrew by boat privately to a solitary place" (Matthew 14:13).

He was looking for a quiet place to get alone and grieve, but once again people follow Him.

I am always touched by the way Jesus is impacted by the brokenness of our world. He weeps over the death of Lazarus, whom He knows He is about to rise from the dead. He is often moved with compassion for the crowds of needy people, as He is in this story. The brokenness of humanity touches the depths of Jesus' tender love, and what I want you to know is that He didn't have to make Himself vulnerable to pain. He could have played it safe in Heaven and avoided all the close and personal encounters with suffering, but He didn't. He is described by Isaiah as being "despised and rejected by men; a man of sorrows and acquainted with grief" (Isaiah 53:3, ESV). To me, this is part of the beauty of Jesus, and it is a moving display of His tenderness. He could have kept Himself invulnerable, but instead He became one of us and entered

> He could have kept Himself invulnerable, but instead He became one of us and entered our vulnerability and suffering. I love Him for that.

our vulnerability and suffering. I love Him for that, and it draws me near to His tender heart.

Second, I see the tenderness of Jesus in this passage in His care for His disciples. He is hurting because of the death of John, but they are hurting too. Remember that many of His followers were once John's followers, so they too are grieving. They have also just come back from a ministry trip, and the crowds are pressing in on them, so He invites them on a retreat to get some rest. Listen, life has a way of wearing us out. Busyness is depleting. And as you have already discovered, there is a relentless list of things that need to be done, and it is tiresome. My to-do list is never done: as soon as I finish with one thing, there is another item to be added. Emails are never finished being answered; you respond to one and you get ten more. Often at conferences I am standing in a restroom answering an email and someone will say to me, "You're answering emails in the bathroom?" But if I don't answer them there, I'll fall even further behind, because when I am at a conference, the emails keep coming. That's the nature of life's demands. And then there is the burden of all the pain, loss, and relentless suffering in the world.

Soul Care has reached hundreds of thousands of people between the book, the conferences, and the eCourse. Nearly every day I receive at least one email or other form of communication from some dear person in desperate need of help. These are people I do not know personally; they have just read the book. Of course, I cannot possibly respond to them all. But I feel the heart of Jesus for them, and sometimes I feel bad I can't do more and that there aren't enough people out there to help the people crying out in need. It also helps me understand how busy and in demand Jesus and His disciples were. Without proper care of our souls, we will be overwhelmed with the unending flood of human need. Jesus sees our limits; Jesus knows our needs and Jesus cares.

The disciples have just been ministering to crowds full of pain—to the sick, the poor, the oppressed, and the demonized. They listened to heartbreaking stories and witnessed people living under the weight of a world full of pain and evil. You know that I travel around the world and do Soul Care Conferences, and everywhere I go people share their stories with me. The stories deplete you: stories of abuse, abandonment, neglect, rejection, heartache, rape, divorce, adultery, betrayal, violence, and every other terrible effect of evil you can imagine. I am incredibly grateful that so often people experience God's presence, power, healing, and freedom—and it is a beautiful thing to behold. But it doesn't take away from the fact that we live in a broken world full of pain that the human heart finds wearisome. The disciples have been ministering under the weight of human brokenness, and Jesus knows that they need a break. They need quiet, rest, retreat, and restoration. As you know, I have taken spiritual retreats for many years. Spiritual retreats are refueling centers for the soul. I couldn't do all the weighty work of Soul Care without regular spiritual retreats. I often hear Jesus saying to me, "Come away with me. Rest awhile." It is the tender voice of invitation to the soul-weary traveler in a world full of pain. He invites you to come and rest in His presence when you are weary, and I know that some of you keenly feel the soul-robbing effects of pain and suffering.

Of course, the disciples' rest is interrupted by another needy crowd, and once again we witness the tenderness of Jesus on display. "So they went away by themselves in a boat to a solitary place. But many who saw them leaving recognized them and ran on foot from all the towns and got there ahead of them. When Jesus landed and saw a large crowd, he had compassion on them, because they were like sheep without a shepherd. So he began teaching them many things" (Mark 6:32-34). You can feel the desperation of the people in the story—running on foot from all the surrounding towns to get a piece of Jesus. You can probably also feel the emotional exhaustion of Jesus and the disciples. They think they are coming to a respite of solitude, and instead they end up in a mob of human need. Sigh.

Do you remember the emotional impact of the day many Americans know simply as 9-1-1? You were all so young; Danielle was only 6. I'm sure you recall some of it; your mother and I remember. The people in the United States were stunned. It was one of those rare moments in life when everyone remembers exactly where they were and what they were doing when they heard the news. I was at the office. We were about to enter a staff meeting and one of our friends from another nearby office came running into our room yelling, "Turn on the TV. We are under attack!" Surreal moment. We turned on the TV and watched in stunned silence as the Twin Towers in New York City burned and collapsed. For the next few days it was as if the world stopped on its axis. Perhaps, for a moment, I glimpsed what it was like to see the world from Jesus' perspective. "He had compassion on them, because they were like sheep without a shepherd." People were devastated, lost, beleaguered, and overwhelmed by fear, pain, loss, and the impact of evil. The truth is that this is always happening in our world around us, but we do not always have eyes to see, ears to hear, or a heart to feel. But Jesus does. So He set aside His tiredness and grief and ministered to a crowd desperate for a tenderhearted shepherd of their souls. This is what Jesus is like, and this is why I love Him.

It was already late in the day, and after teaching for a while, the disciples once again asked Jesus to get rid of the people. At this point, the disciples had not learned how to draw upon God's supernatural resources for compassionate care in a burdensome world. You must learn that, as I have had to, or we cannot continue to care for the overwhelming needs of this suffering-infused planet—and even then we have limits and need breaks of replenishment. God is an endless source of compassion, but if we rely on our own resources of compassion, we will burn out. It is simply too much for us to bear without fresh encounters with the tenderness of Jesus. "This is a remote place," they said, "and it's already very late. Send the people away so that they can go to the surrounding countryside and villages and buy themselves something to eat" (Mark 6:35, 36). This seems like a reasonable idea to the entire ministry team—except for Jesus. He sees it as a unique opportunity: "You give them something to eat" (Mark 6:37). Can't you picture their faces? They are probably hoping He is joking, but seeing no sign of humor, they begin to protest. First, it would cost too much money. Second, where would they find food enough for such a huge crowd? They are in a remote place, remember, because they were going away on a retreat.

Jesus does a quick resource assessment and discovers they have access to a grand total of five loaves of bread and two fish to feed five thousand people (and this, the Bible tells us, only counted the men). Jesus factors in the neediness of the "sheep," the weariness of the hour, the tenderness He feels, and His Father's power, and He has everyone sit down for a remarkable feast: "Taking the five loaves and the two fish and looking up to heaven, he gave thanks and broke the loaves. Then he gave them to his disciples to set before the people. He also divided up the two fish among them all. They all ate and were satisfied, and the disciples picked up twelve basketfuls of broken pieces of bread and fish" (Mark 6:41-43).

I love Jesus' complete confidence in His Father. He simply knows that His Father will multiply the food and provide for the crowd, so He gives thanks for all to see. But mostly, I am deeply moved by the loving compassion of Jesus throughout this story. He demonstrates His love for the disciples in their weariness and grief by taking them on retreat. He displays His tenderness with the crowd by teaching them, even though He is exhausted, because He sees the desperation in their hearts. Then Jesus expresses His gentle love for them by putting on a feast from a morsel of scraps because they were tired and in a remote place. They were tired, but what about Him? The self-lessness of Jesus is essential to His displays of tenderness. We cannot be selfish and tenderhearted. Selflessness and tender-ness go hand in hand. I think the tenderness of Jesus comes back again at the end of the story when He brings the disciples into the miracle. He has them hand out the loaves, they get to see it multiply in their hands, they pick up the scraps, and they witness how powerful the miracle was. I tell you, from firsthand experience, that no matter how tired I am doing ministry, when the power of God is on undisputed display it energizes my weary soul.

After I left South Shore Community Church and started traveling a lot more, I would often get ready to leave for a trip and say to Mom, "I can't keep doing this." It was the wear and tear of the constant departures and life on the road. But the more I traveled, and the more I saw God changing lives, doing miracles, and healing bodies and souls, the more I was energized and accepted this call on my life. I have seen Jesus change so many lives, children; I wish you could have been there with me for all that I have seen Jesus do and all I have experienced.

This is what Jesus is like. So compelling. So compassionate. The more I get to know Him, the more I am moved to love Him.

## Tenderness to the Hopeless

I know that some of you have had bouts of depression or experienced shrouds of darkness. Mom wrestled with that some, too, especially earlier in our marriage. It happens to many people in life for a variety of reasons. When Mom and I went through our first and most severe marriage crisis we both felt hopeless. We were talking every night, doing everything we knew to do, yet not making any progress. I remember one or both of us expressing how hopeless we felt, often after these seemingly fruitless discussions. There were times I felt hopeless when I went through the worst ministry crisis in my life. You probably don't remember too much about those years, as I said earlier, but when people were attacking me almost weekly for about five years, it was incredibly painful, and it felt like the church was completely destabilized. I had spent my whole life building up the church, and it felt like it was being dismantled by the enemy and some divisive people. God redeemed both of those dark seasons in my life in ways I could never have imagined. Soul Care was the result of the marriage crisis, and it has been used by God to help literally hundreds of thousands of people around the world. Only God! The ministry crisis became an avenue to develop spiritual authority in me which resulted in a release of Jesus' power in my ministry that has impacted thousands of people and given me great joy. I wouldn't trade those two crises for anything in the world because of how God redeemed them. But in the midst of them, there were times I felt utterly hopeless. It is part of the human condition.

The last story I want to look at comes from the Gospel of Luke and examines two people who are being crushed by some hopeless circumstances. The two stories are intertwined because they overlap.

One day, Jesus, the ultimate protagonist of the human storyline, again finds Himself in the middle of a crowd—one full of people in need. One of the people who came that day was a man named Jairus, and he came in desperation on behalf of his daughter. "Then a man named Jairus, a synagogue leader, came and fell at Jesus' feet, pleading with him to come to his house because his only daughter, a girl of about twelve, was dying" (Luke 8:41, 42).

Mom and I have been fortunate that all of you have been in good health. Craig, of course, has diabetes, but we have been privileged to live in the US where there is insulin readily available. I remember when Craig first got diagnosed with diabetes, I went on a missions trip to Senegal with a team from church. Doctor John was leading the trip, and one day I was testing people's sugars. I came across a little boy, probably 5 or 6, about Craig's age at the time, and his sugar was over 800 (instead of the desired 80 to 120). That's what Craig's sugar was when we discovered he had diabetes and took him to Children's Hospital in Boston. Well, I knew enough about diabetes to know this little guy in Senegal had it. I told John his number and asked him, "What will they do?" He frowned and simply said, "Nothing." I asked what would happen, and John said, "He will die young." Imagine if that was us? Imagine the lengths to which Mom and I would go to seek healing for one of you?

That's Jairus's story. His only daughter is dying, and he has nowhere to turn—until he hears about Jesus. Can you imagine the hope that people must have felt when they listened to the healing stories of Jesus? Can you imagine the hope that was conveyed every time someone spoke His name, every time someone told a testimony of His healing power, His tender touch? This is one of the sad parts of living in a land of plenty with a Western worldview: Jesus is often our last resort, and we know so little of His power compared to other places in the world. This is why I have spent my life in passionate pursuit of revival. I don't want to settle for a powerless version of Christianity. You know that in places where Jesus' power is still on display there is much less deconstruction needed and talked about. Powerless Christianity is not biblical; it is

Powerless Christianity is not biblical; it is *religious*. It doesn't draw people in, it repels people.

*religious*. It doesn't draw people in, it repels people. It often fosters an atmosphere where people argue for their version of the truth, love less, and judge more. It most often does not represent Jesus well. In the New Testament there is no authentic proclamation of the gospel of the Kingdom without a demonstration of power. If Jesus is truly the same yesterday, today, and forever, as Scripture says (Hebrews 13:8), then Jesus still does what Jesus always did.

But Jairus isn't the only one in the story with a desperate situation. As Jesus starts toward Jairus's house to heal his daughter, a woman with a hopeless medical condition sneaks up on Him. "As Jesus was on his way, the crowds almost crushed him. And a woman was there who had been subject to bleeding for twelve years, but no one could heal her" (Luke 8:42, 43). Mark's Gospel reveals that she had spent all her money trying to resolve her medical condition but had only gotten worse (Mark 5:26). Ponder the weightiness of that situation. You are so desperate for healing that you are willing to spend your entire life savings to get well, but nothing works. You are left broke and brokenhearted; that is a surefire formula for despair. Then one day she heard about Jesus.

Can you imagine being so desperate, and then hearing the stories about One who heals so many? So she seeks Him out and finds Him! In a crowd, of course. She picks and weaves her way through the crowd and grabs a corner of Jesus' garment. But her faith is so rich, so real, so fervent, it becomes the conduit of God's power, and she is instantly healed. "She came up behind him and touched the edge of his cloak, and immediately her bleeding stopped" (Luke 8:44). She must have known it, and she hoped to slip away unnoticed. Did you ever wonder why she came in this covert manner and tried to slip away without notice with her healing? I think the answer to that question is precisely why Jesus seeks her out.

In a comical exchange, Jesus asks the disciples who touched Him. "'Who touched me?' Jesus asked. When they all denied it, Peter said, 'Master, the people are crowding and pressing against you.' But Jesus said, 'Someone has touched me; I know that power has gone out from me'" (Luke 8:45, 46). Jesus is searching for the garment grabber, but the culprit is trying to sneak out. Peter chimes in with the obvious observation that in a crowd that is nearly crushing them to death, it's pretty hard to determine exactly who has touched Him! Jesus explains that someone touched Him, and they know who they are, because power has gone out from Him. He felt the power leave His body as it accomplished its work.

That is when the woman realizes she needs to come clean. "Then the woman, seeing that she could not go unnoticed, came trembling and fell at his feet. In the presence of all the people, she told why she had touched him and how she had been instantly healed. Then he said to her, 'Daughter, your faith has healed you. Go in peace'" (Luke 8:47, 48). I love this story.

The woman is terrified, which is why she is hiding. She is likely terrified because she has been sneaky, and she is afraid of getting caught and called out. But the reason she was sneaky is because she was afraid to begin with. I would venture a guess that she was afraid, at least in part, because she was a woman in a man's world. I know today, though we have made progress, we still live in a male-dominated world, especially within the walls of many conservative churches. That saddens me for you, and especially for you girls: Danielle, Courtney, and Darcy. But Jesus isn't like that. He has tenderness for women, children, and men, and He treats everyone with dignity and honor alike.

But I also suspect that a large part of her fear is connected to her illness. In the Jewish society, to prevent the spread of illnesses that could wipe out a fledgling nomadic people, God inaugurated certain rules. If you were experiencing a blood discharge, you were to declare yourself "unclean" so the discharge would not spread to many. It was the earliest form of social distancing! But when you have to constantly self-declare as unclean, you begin to feel dirty, unwanted, and unloved. So the woman crossed social and religious barriers to touch Jesus, a holy man, and she was afraid of the ramifications if she would be caught. She just wanted to sneak by, grab His garment, get better, and get on with life as it used to be! She is afraid to ask for help and afraid to get caught. But Jesus won't let her stealthy operation go unnoticed.

Jesus has no judgment to offer her. Jesus never has judgment for people who approach Him with faith and humility, no matter who they are or what they have done. I love the statement in John's gospel that follows the most famous verse in the Bible: "For God so loved the world that he gave his one and only Son, that whoever believes in him shall not perish but have eternal life. For God did not send his Son into the world to condemn the world, but to save the world through him" (John 3:16, 17). Jesus didn't come to condemn the world; Jesus came to save us. Whenever you see the church acting in condemning, judgmental ways, please know that this does not represent Jesus well. He is not like that.

You know I love *A Christmas Carol* by Charles Dickens. I read it every year. I read it to you when you were little. When Scrooge is talking to the Ghost of Christmas Present, he tells the ghost that he has deprived poor people of the right to gather for dinner out on Sundays. He is referring to the old blue laws that were connected to the Sabbath and shut everything down on Sunday. But the ghost objects and says he isn't depriving the poor of this pleasure. "'There are some upon this earth of yours,' returned the Spirit, 'who lay claim to know us, and who do their deeds of passion, pride, ill-will, hatred, envy, bigotry, and selfishness in our name, who are as strange to us and all our kith and kin, as if they had never lived. Remember that, and charge their doings on themselves, not us'" (Dickens, *A Christmas Carol,* Stave 3). That is a wise piece of advice. Don't confuse the judgmental misdeeds of those who claim to know Christ with Jesus Himself. Don't judge Jesus by those who fail to represent Him well yet claim His name.

> Don't confuse the judgmental misdeeds of those who claim to know Christ with Jesus Himself.

Jesus is full of truth and full of grace. He looks at my life and yours and points out our wrongdoings. But He has no judgment or condemnation to offer. Jesus never reveals sin to us to judge us, but to free us with His tender displays of grace: to change us. Even if you are not ready to change and choose God's path in some area of your life, know this: Jesus still loves you, and He longs for your best. There is nothing you can do to make Jesus love you less; there is nothing you can do to make Jesus love you more.

After she tells her story, Jesus offers her tender words of life: "Daughter, your faith has healed you. Go in peace." "Daughter" is a gentle, kind expression. Jesus is clearly not old enough to be her father, but she is His daughter because she is a child of God, and He is the Ancient of Days (as Scripture says). She is loved, and she is home; she is safe and she is saved in Jesus' presence. The word He uses for healed is the Greek word for "saved." The salvation of Jesus extends to all the effects of sin. All that sin has distorted in the world, Jesus seeks to restore. All that sin and evil have robbed us of, Jesus came to overturn. This is the Gospel of the Kingdom. The Kingdom is the reversal of everything that went wrong with the world when sin entered the world; it is the restoration of the way things were supposed to be. So when you see oppression in the world, it is because of sin; when you see Jesus advancing His Kingdom, He is restoring things to their original intention.

I think one of the reasons Jesus sought this woman out, and would not let her quietly slip away, is because she needed more than physical healing. She need healing for the rejection she felt because she was labeled "unclean." She had come to believe that she was unclean, unacceptable, unlovable to others. Jesus wanted to pronounce her "clean." She was healed, saved, delivered, freed, acceptable, and loved, and no longer did she need to slink along at the edge of humanity feeling unwanted. So Jesus called her out and waited for her so He could restore to her all that evil had stolen. This is the beautiful tenderness of Jesus; this is how He sees you and how He treats you. Don't let anyone's mistreatments, judgments, or misrepresentations confuse you about the way Jesus is.

As Jesus was proclaiming peace to the woman, devastating news came from Jairus's household. "While Jesus was still speaking, someone came from the house of Jairus, the synagogue leader. 'Your daughter is dead,' he said. 'Don't bother the teacher anymore'" (Luke 8:49). Jairus knew she was dying, but so long as she was still alive, he reasoned, there was hope. But this was the end—the end of her life, the end of his hopes and dreams for his little girl. There is no recovery from this.

Fortunately, Jesus overhears the news, and He intervenes. "Hearing this, Jesus said to Jairus, 'Don't be afraid; just believe, and she will be healed'" (Luke 8:50). It is nearly impossible to overestimate the importance of faith in the Bible. Did you notice what Jesus said to the woman? "Your faith has healed you." And here, to Jairus, Jesus says, "Just believe, and she will be healed." One of the most important things to do on your spiritual journey is to develop faith. You likely know that I wrote an entire book on that subject, *Deep Faith,* and it's a book I think can help you on your faith development journey. I also recommended to you the book *Miracles Today,* by Craig Keener. Few books that I have read in the past decade have strengthened my faith like that one. I will mention one other book that has helped my faith. The book is by George Müller, *Answers to Prayer.* He was a man of remarkable faith; I don't think I've ever read anyone who had faith like Müller, and his life has helped and challenged me. We must intentionally develop our faith because the world is constantly undermining our trust in God.

If we are going to cultivate deeper faith, we must strengthen our grip on the goodness of God. We will not trust God if we do not believe He is good. Trust is the bridge to intimacy—we can never go deeper in intimacy than our trust can carry us. Understanding and experiencing Jesus' tenderness is so important because when we know Jesus' tender love, we will trust Him—even in life's darkest hours.

Fortunately, Jairus had just watched this woman's healing, and that helped him hang onto faith. This is the power of testimonies: they strengthen our faith. The story, as you might expect, has a happy ending. "When he arrived at the house of Jairus, he did not let anyone go in with him except Peter, John, and James, and the child's father and mother. Meanwhile, all the people were wailing and mourning for her. 'Stop wailing,' Jesus said. 'She is not dead but asleep.' They laughed at him, knowing that she was dead. But he took her by the hand and said, 'My child, get up!' Her spirit returned, and at once she stood up. Then Jesus told them to give her something to eat. Her parents were astonished, but he ordered them not to tell anyone what had happened" (Luke 8:51-56).

One of the things you will notice as you read the Gospels is that Jesus is often trying to keep a lid on His popularity—and that was not easy! He exhorts people frequently not to tell anyone about the miracles He has done. Part of that is because it is not His time yet to die on the cross, and He knows the more the word spreads, the quicker the spiritual leaders will seek to execute Him. Scholars often call this "the Messianic Secret." This also why He tells the people the little girl is not dead but asleep. Of course, He knows that He will raise her from the dead, that she is just temporarily taking a little nap from life, soon to be awakened. Notice again how Jesus makes Himself vulnerable: they all laugh at Him because they know she is dead. Jesus subjects Himself to ridicule, abuse, and even crucifixion because of His love for us. He chooses to identify with us in our weakness so we can share in His power.

I love the way Jesus raises the little girl from the dead. He addresses her tenderly: "My child." And He commands her to rise: "Get up!" One of the things I often do when I read the Gospels is try to picture the scene in my mind. Being a parent, I imagine what it would be like if one of you had died, and how I would feel if Jesus spoke these words to you and I saw you raise from the dead. Simply over-whelming. If that were your little girl, your heart would be forever bound to Jesus.

> I love the way Jesus raises the little girl from the dead. He addresses her tenderly: "My child."

Do you remember the time Danielle almost drowned and Cousin Nick saved her? Imagine how differently life would have gone for the rest of us if Nick hadn't saved her. You know that every time I see Nick or even think about him, I think about the time he saved Danielle. I always think of Nick with great fondness because of what he did.

I love Jesus' last act of tenderness in this passage. He tells the parents to give her something to eat. He is practical and concerned with our basic human needs. Just as He wanted the crowd to be fed before they headed home, He wants the little girl to eat now that she is alive and feeling better!

We need to experience Jesus' tenderness, not just learn about it. A lot of people have read the books I have written. When I am speaking at a conference, often someone comes to me and says, "I feel like I know you because I've read your books and you write so personally." And it is true that I write openly, honestly, and vulnerably. But it is not true that they know me. They know about me. They have read about me. But they don't know me. Not like you know me, or Mom knows me, or one of my friends knows me. It's the same with Jesus; it isn't enough to read the Bible and know about Him. We must get to know Him intimately, and that means we must experience Him. The more we experience the tender acts of Jesus in our own lives, the more we will trust Him, love Him, and follow Him wherever He leads. This is what I pray and hope for you!

## Experience

Linger with Jesus. Come to Him as you are. You may come desperately on behalf of someone else in need. You may have needs of your own that seem so weighty and troubling. Perhaps you come with a weariness from all of life's demands and burdens. Whatever state of heart and soul you find yourself in, come to Jesus just as you are and present yourself to Him. Be honest. Tell Him what you feel, what you're going through, what you're experiencing. Then just sit in His presence in stillness and linger with Him.

Listen and linger, receive and rest.

*"No friend sympathizes so tenderly with his friend in affliction as Jesus Christ does with his friends. . . . He feels all our sorrows, needs, and burdens as his own."*

– JOHN FLAVEL[3]

Three
———

# THE TENDER WORDS OF JESUS

Children, do you remember when Mom used to talk to little kids who had their feelings hurt? If someone said something that was hurtful, she would ask the little one, "Well, is that true about you?" And the little one would say, "No!" Mom would say, "Then they are just wrong." It was pretty funny to watch little kids interact with her in this way. But, of course, the reality is that even if someone says something to you that is not true, it still hurts. Words hurt.

I had someone blast me on social media not long ago, and they said some things about me that simply were not true. This person had something near one million followers and literally thousands of people jumped on the bandwagon maligning me. What they said was completely wrong. But it still hurt.

Fortunately, I knew what to do with it—this wasn't my first rodeo with public attacks. I blessed the person who was cursing me, didn't defend myself, and went to Jesus. His tender words often have been a source of comfort and healing in my soul.

In this chapter I want to look with you at the way Jesus expresses tenderness through some of His teachings. There are, of course, far too many teachings for me to include all of them. So I will look at just a few passages that pull back the curtain and give you a peak into the heart of the Savior.

## The Good News

Jesus describes the message that He proclaims as "good news." Mark writes, "After John was put in prison, Jesus went into Galilee, proclaiming the good news of God. 'The time has come,' he said. 'The kingdom of God has come near. Repent and believe the good news!'" (Mark 1:14, 15). This is the central message of Jesus: the good news or gospel of the Kingdom of God.

This is arguably the most important thing to recognize about the message of Jesus, and He self-describes it as good news. Don't miss this: that is what Jesus thought about the message He preached. Think about receiving good news from any corridor of life: it is welcomed news, it is received with joy, it produces gladness and hope. This is the nature of good news! This isn't like watching the nightly news, which is saturated with sad and depressing sound bites that bring a pall of gloom over the most optimistic soul. Jesus' news report is entirely the opposite. So if you understand the message of Jesus in a way that doesn't produce gladness and joy, you likely misunderstand what He is saying.

When the message you hear from Christians or the church sounds like bad news, it is likely a distorted version of what Jesus taught. Don't take other people's word for what Jesus taught; take a fresh look at the Gospels. Read Jesus' words for yourself and look at them through the lens Jesus gave us—it is a message of good news! I have to tell you that I read the Gospels nearly every day, and I have done so since my early twenties. One of the reasons I read the Gospels so much is because I am committed to following Jesus, so I want to saturate my life with His words. I never want to get far from Jesus. I read the rest of the Bible too, but I focus most on Jesus because He is the hero of the story. The most important reason I have turned so frequently to the gospels is because I love Jesus; He is truly the most compelling person I have encountered. It is the good news about Jesus that has captured my heart.

People flocked to Jesus to hear Him preach because His message was good news and was accompanied by powerful miracles. People who were hated and despised came in droves because His message was full of love. People forgotten and abandoned by society fought through crowds to catch a glimpse of Jesus because His words were so rich and full of acceptance. Jesus gave people who were far from God hope that they could draw near. He helped unwanted outcasts feel like they mattered to God. He brokered hope to the spiritually disqualified who were scorned by the religious leaders and haunted by a lifestyle of bad decisions, yet they were welcomed by Jesus. He tenderly touched the untouchables. He graciously loved the unlovable. Jesus gave hope to the despairing, courage to the fearful, liberty to the demonized, healing to the sick, and peace to the anxious.

> Jesus gave hope to the despairing, courage to the fearful, liberty to the demonized, healing to the sick, and peace to the anxious.

There was no one too far from God for Jesus to lead them home. There was no one too unclean for Him to offer purifying hope. There was no one too diseased for Him to heal. There was no one too demonized for Him to deliver. There was no one too hated for Him to love. There was no one beyond Jesus' reach; no one hopeless in Jesus' hands. This is why Jesus' message was good news—good news to all who heard and understood.

Too often the message you hear from Christians is a message of religion and not actually the good news of the Kingdom. It is a message that leaves people feeling guilt, shame, and even more burdened. It often comes with heaviness and oppression. But that isn't the message of Jesus. Jesus' message was the good news of the Kingdom of God.

Let's talk about the Kingdom of God. I spent an entire chapter discussing the Kingdom in my book *Spiritual Authority,* so you can read more there. But let me give a quick overview of Kingdom theology. The Bible teaches that God created people in His image, and He gave them a kingdom; they were to have dominion over the earth. But sadly, humanity sinned—men and women rebelled against God, and the world was forever changed by the presence of evil. The world is now broken, and it doesn't work the way God intended it to operate. Now we have injustice and oppression, sickness and death, wars and persecution, natural disasters and environmental problems. We also have relational problems, addictions, and destructive patterns of behavior that are hard to break. Yet God loved us, despite our rejection of Him, so He pursued us. Like a jilted lover He sought to win back the heart of His adulterous bride. In the Old Testament God chose Israel to be the object of His affections. He sought to win over the Hebrew people, and they were to represent Him to the rest of the world.

But sadly, in this love story, they continued to rebel and reject Him despite His entreaties. Still, God wouldn't quit pursuing humanity, the object of His unwarranted affection. He sent them prophets and leaders to call them back home. And when all His efforts were met with unrequited love, He sent Jesus.

The Bible, in so many ways, tells the remarkable story of a God whose love will not quit in the face of continual rejection by the people He created. That was my own story, too. I grew up going to church. Grandma came from a Protestant family, Grandpa was Catholic. Back in those days, there was even a greater gulf between Protestants and Catholics than there is today, and neither of their parents approved of them being together, so they eloped. In the earlier years, when your Uncle Ken and I were still young, Grandpa would go to the early Catholic Mass and then he would come to church with Uncle Ken, Grandma, and I because he wanted to be with the family. So as early as I can remember, I went to church. When I was a little boy, I went to a little Christian and Missionary Alliance Church in Clinton Corners, New York. I don't remember much about it, but I do remember one of my Sunday School teachers who always made me feel welcome and loved. When you look back on your life, you can always see people God sent your way who made deposits of God's goodness in your life. Reflect on that; it is one of the ways Jesus' tenderness is revealed to us. But Jesus wasn't really the center of my life through my years of growing up; He was on the edges.

When I was 17 I started dating a girl in our church, and this made church more interesting to me! A couple of years later, she broke up with me. It was mostly my fault because I was too selfish, and I had never grappled with my self-centeredness and its toxic influence on others. Most of us don't realize the damage done by our self-centeredness. On my way home from her house after she broke up with me, I pulled off to the side of the road and cried out to God. Much to my surprise, I sensed God speaking to me. It was the first time I felt like God was talking to me. It wasn't an audible voice, but somehow or other in my inner being I knew what God was saying: "This is the way you have treated me. I loved you, but you rejected me." I saw an image of Jesus in my mind's eye; He was calling me to come to Him, and I was holding my hand up, pushing Him away to the edges of my life. I repented and invited Jesus into the center of my life. I said, "From now on, you lead, I'll follow." From that day on, I have sought to follow Jesus sincerely in all things. When I prayed that prayer, I encountered Jesus' love for the first time in my life. So many of my questions, though still unanswered, became less important in the experience of Jesus' deep love.

Jesus came to show us the Father, to reveal what He is truly like, to demonstrate God's love for us, to win our heart's affection, and to pave the way for us to be forgiven and reconciled to God so we can live a new life of fullness and freedom. The author of Hebrews writes, "In the past God spoke to our ancestors through the prophets at many times and in various ways, but in these last days he has spoken to us by his Son, whom he appointed heir of all things, and through whom also he made the universe. The Son is the radiance of God's glory and the exact representation of his being, sustaining all things by his powerful word. After he had provided purification for sins, he sat down at the right hand of the Majesty in heaven" (Hebrews 1:1-3). Jesus came to represent the Father perfectly to us; He came to purify us and reconcile us to God. And He came to win back the rights to the Kingdom for humanity and to hand us the keys to that Kingdom.

Scripture says that Satan is now the ruler of the air (Ephesians 2:2), the god of this world (2 Corinthians 4:4). He usurped the keys of the Kingdom from humanity by leading us into rebellion against God, but Jesus came as the second Adam (1 Corinthians 15:45-47). He was tempted in every way as we are, yet He did not sin (Hebrews 4:15). He defeated Satan with His perfect obedience to the Father, and He overcame death by His resurrection because no sin could be held against Him to keep Him in the grave. Jesus defeated our enemies: sin, sickness, death, and Satan, and He won back the keys to the Kingdom. He then handed the keys back to their original owners: those He created in His image.

If you have been listening to me over the years, you have heard me say this before: the Kingdom of God is the reversal of everything that went wrong with the world when sin entered the world. It is the restoration of the way things are supposed to be. It includes forgiveness and reconciliation to God, but it doesn't end there. Read the Gospels and you will see Jesus proclaim this good news of the Kingdom, and then He heals the sick (see, for example, Matthew 4:23-25). This is the Kingdom breaking through the tyrannical rule of Hell on earth and overthrowing sickness. Jesus preached the Kingdom, and then He cast out demons. When the Kingdom comes, Hell loses its grip on people. This is the beauty of the message and ministry of Jesus—this is the good news! Jesus preached the Kingdom, then He fed the hungry and called the church to care for the poor. There was no poverty before sin entered the world, and there will be no poverty in Heaven. God has no lack; the world has lack because of sin—fear, greed, selfishness, and power-hungry pride lead to poverty. Jesus preached the Gospel of the Kingdom, then He began to overthrow injustice, leading justice to victory. Injustice and oppression are byproducts of evil, but there was no injustice before sin, and there will be no injustice in Heaven.

This is why it is called good news. It is good news for everyone when God's desire for goodness is manifest in your life on earth, when Satan's grip of evil is dismantled in the wake of the coming Kingdom of God. This is the message Jesus proclaimed; this was the work Jesus did. This is what Jesus is like.

> True repentance is liberating, freeing, transforming, and life-giving. It is restorative and reconciling.

Now I want you to notice something that may seem odd at first and confuses a lot of people about the good news: repentance is directly linked to this message of good news. Most people do not associate repentance with good news! Repentance is often seen through the dark lens of religion. It is seen as heavy, weighty, dark, and discouraging. It is often associated with judgment and condemnation. But that isn't the feel of true biblical repentance. True repentance is liberating, freeing, transforming, and life-giving. It is restorative and reconciling. True repentance gets us out of the moral ditch and into right alignment with God where we experience freedom and fullness. It's when we get back into alignment with God and sense His presence, tenderness, and love. I told the story above about when I repented of my rejection of Jesus and He poured out His love in my heart. It wasn't a terrible feeling of guilt, shame, and condemnation; it was an awakening to my selfishness which produced true remorse and led to an encounter with Jesus' tender affections and His liberating forgiveness. It was the best day of my young life. That's why it is good news!

In Acts 3, after Peter and John healed a paralyzed man in Jesus' name, a large crowd gathered and Peter preached to them. He said, "Repent, then, and turn to God, so that your sins may be wiped out, that times of refreshing may come from the Lord" (Acts 3:19). I love that. That is true repentance. It wipes away our sin and leads to times of refreshing in the Lord. It brings us back into alignment with God so His Spirit can flow over our lives in times of refreshing and renewal. That's why it is good news!

Not that long ago, Mom, Craig, and I were in England, and I stepped off the sidewalk and into the road. Unfortunately, I looked the wrong way because I am so used to traffic in the US coming from the right. I stepped right into oncoming traffic, but Mom reached out and grabbed me and pulled me back. That correction was for my good because my choice was leading to some unwanted, disastrous consequences! I didn't feel bad that she corrected me—I was thankful! I needed it; it literally saved my life. That's how biblical repentance works. Life works better when we go God's way. Jesus models God's way and calls us into God's way so we can experience the abundant life God offers.

I have to tell you, most of the time when repentance feels like a burden to me, it is because I do not want to go God's way. I am doing my own thing, and I don't want to bring myself into alignment with God. I want to push God to the edges, and I want to put me at the center. I want what I want, and I am fighting against God; it is that self-centered pull within me that causes me to resist God and rebel against Him. But when I am struggling to say yes to God, when I am fighting for my own way, I do not feel free. I feel burdened and restless, I feel irritated and aggravated, I feel anxious and uneasy. When I finally surrender and say yes to God, the burden lifts, peace comes, and I feel restored. There is no peace without surrender; there is no freedom without bringing myself into alignment with God. When I refuse to go God's way, I am swimming against the tide of the way life works, and it is burdensome to do so. Jesus, in His tenderness, calls me home, and He does it because He loves me and wants my best.

As I said, like the four of you, I grew up going to church, but I wasn't following Jesus. By most human standards, I was a decent person. The problem with humanity is not that we sin, but that we are sinners. That's why we need a Savior. Being a sinner simply means we have a propensity to go our own way, to do our own thing; we have an enormous bias toward self. This is our *self-life*—we are self-reliant, self-dependent, self-centered, self-protective, and often selfish. We want to make our own decisions, do our own thing, and push God out of the center of our lives. Ironically, I have found that the more I feed this self-life the more miserable I become. The only time I am truly miserable is when I am making life too much about me. It is too much about my needs, my wants, my desires, my opinions, and my feelings. When I am focused on my wants, my needs, and my desires in marriage with Mom, for example, I am never happy. But when I focus on loving Mom and doing the things Jesus calls me to do, I find my life is much more fulfilling. Jesus called us to pick up our cross daily and follow Him (Luke 9:23) because this is the way to life. Repentance is good news because we start to see the Kingdom breaking into our lives and relationships. Life works the way Heaven intended it should. Selfishness is a byproduct of human rebellion against God. Dying to self, saying yes to Jesus and no to our self-bias—these are the pathways to abundant life. And we start to see the goodness of God and the tender affections of Jesus like we have never seen.

This is the life I long for you to experience since I love you all so much.

## An Invitation to the Weary

Religion always puts heavy burdens on people. The Pharisees and Jewish leaders of Jesus' day put a lot of religious requirements on people. The requirements went way beyond God's commands and were weighty on people. It was like trying to carry around a heavy rock all day long wherever you went; you could never put it down, you could never let it go. That is how religion is: it is weighty, oppressive, and burdensome. It encumbers people with guilt, shame, and condemnation.

> Religion always puts heavy burdens on people. The Pharisees and Jewish leaders of Jesus' day put a lot of religious requirements on people.

It makes it too much about us and not enough about Jesus, and it is a soul-wearying endeavor.

But Jesus isn't like that. In one of the most famous passages in the Bible, Jesus interacts with a religious leader named Nicodemus (John 3). Nicodemus tells Jesus that people know He has come from God because of the miracles He is doing. Jesus gave him a reply that seemed to come out of left field: "Very truly I tell you, no one can see the kingdom of God without being born again" (John 3:3). Born again? Nicodemus is totally confused by this metaphor, and he asks how one can reenter their mother's womb. Jesus clarifies that He is not speaking of another physical birth, but a spiritual one. Just as we are born into our biological family through the birth canal, we must be born into God's family through the Spirit. Through faith in Jesus we are born into God's family, and the Spirit of God now dwells within us. This is the key to true life change. It isn't about trying harder or doing more. It is about learning how to develop an intimate, empowering relationship with the Spirit of God within us. We have to learn how to yield ourselves to Him and allow Him to empower our choices for a better life.

Religion makes it about what you do to try to make God happy. You have to do more, be better, quit doing the wrong things, and start doing the right things. Pick up your rock and lug it wherever you go! Religion always goes beyond God's standards and creates new, added burdens. The Bible, for example, says not to get drunk. You don't have to look too hard in this world to figure out why God would say this. You have seen the pain caused by drunkenness—drunken driving deaths, family dysfunction, abuse, and shame. But legalism takes God's standard and, in the name of fear and control, goes beyond what God says and tells people "you cannot drink." It keeps adding to the standards of God to control people because of fear. Jesus called people to stop relying on themselves (to repent) and turn to Him (believe), and He would forgive them for wrongs and give them His Spirit to live out a more fulfilling life. God's Presence will be with you, He says, in you, and the Spirit of God will lead, guide, help, comfort, and empower you to follow God's ways, which bring abundant life. No religion. No heavy burdens. No added requirements. No need to "try harder, do better, and good luck to you in the end." No guilt, shame, or condemnation. Rather, an invitation to relational intimacy that produces authentic life change from within through the indwelling Holy Spirit.

Religion substitutes learned behavior for authentic relationship. We have to do the right things to please God and avoid doing the wrong things. We have to read our Bible and pray to be a good Christian. We have to go to church and help the poor. We can't drink, smoke, lust, or yell at our family. But in reality, all Jesus wants from us is that we humbly invite Him to the center and learn to do life with Him. Keep saying yes, keep being honest, keep humbling ourselves before Him, and He will do the rest.

John's Gospel ends this conversation between Jesus and Nicodemus with the world's most famous verse. There is some scholarly debate as to whether these are Jesus' words or John's words. I think they were probably from Jesus, but either way the words are powerful. "For God so loved the world that he gave his one and only Son, that whoever believes in him shall not perish but have eternal life. For God did not send his Son into the world to condemn the world, but to save the world through him" (John 3:16, 17). Jesus came to break the heavy yoke of religion; He didn't come to condemn but to save. He didn't come to judge but to release us from judgment. He didn't come to burden but to carry the load. He didn't come to scold us but to accept us into His family just as we are. As Courtney's tattoo says, "Come as you are." You don't need to change before you can come; you come to Him for change so you can experience the best life has to offer with eternity waiting in the wings.

This religious heaviness is the backdrop for Jesus' message of good news about the liberating impact of the Kingdom's arrival. Because of the weightiness of religion and the burdens of a fallen world, Jesus said to you and me, "Come to me, all you who are weary and burdened, and I will give you rest. Take my yoke upon you and learn from me, for I am gentle and humble in heart, and you will find rest for your souls.

> These are some of Jesus' most beautiful words of hope and affection.
> He invites you to come when you are weary.

For my yoke is easy and my burden is light" (Matthew 11:28-30). These are some of Jesus' most beautiful words of hope and affection.

He invites you to come when you are weary. Life has a way of wearing us down and wearing us out. Sometimes we are burdened by a sense of guilt and shame. It may be because of religion laying false guilt upon us, but often it is just because we fall short and feel bad about it. I have done things and said things that have been hurtful to you and to Mom; it is, unfortunately, part of being a sinful person in a broken world. All families hurt each other because they live together. When I have hurt you or Mom with my words, for example, I consciously try to sincerely apologize. Darcy, you wrote to me one day and said that you apologized to someone you had hurt, and you said you learned that from me because I always apologized to you guys. That meant a lot to me. No one is ever going to be perfect this side of Heaven, but we ought to be humble enough to say we are sorry and admit we are wrong. It makes a big difference in relationships when we do our best to own our part and mend broken fences. Humility produces reconciliation with God and others. Humility is the mother of all virtue. So I not only apologize to you if I say something hurtful, I also take that wrongdoing to Jesus and ask for His forgiveness as well. I am not burdened by guilt or shame because of Jesus' love and forgiveness. But though I don't feel shame, I have plenty of regrets in life; there are many things I would do differently if I could do life over. Regret is just part of growing wise—you regret what you have done because you have developed enough wisdom to know if you could do it over, you would do so differently.

It isn't just the religious burdens Jesus is concerned with. It's the life burdens as well. Sometimes life is burdensome because of all the things we have to do. Your to-do list is never done. There are always more rooms to clean, lawns to mow, cars to maintain, calls to make, emails to answer, days to work, bills to pay, doctors to visit, broken things to fix, and texts to send. I can't tell you how many times I write a to-do list and feel a momentary twinge of pressure inside. *Oh my gosh, can I get it all done on time?* In my case, a lot of it is self-imposed pressure: for example, no one forces me to write a book, but it is on my list, and I start feeling pressure to get it done. Even writing this book! I already wrote one book in the summer of 2022, and I had the idea that I should also write this book on the tenderness of Jesus for you, and I outlined it, was excited about it, and felt some pressure inside to get it done! I have no deadline that it must be done by, but there was this little internal pressure mounting. This is one of the reasons why, every day, I pray through my to-do list: to bring Jesus into all the weighty pressures of life and release life's burdens to Him, because He cares. You too have felt the weariness of living in a demanding world.

Sometimes we feel pressure to please others: family, friends, coworkers, bosses, people around us. We feel pressure to please people or at least to not disappoint people. You have felt pressure at times to please Mom and me. I will love you even if I am not happy with a choice you make, but it is a natural human inclination to please those we love. We even feel pressure sometimes to please people we do not have a close relationship with. More burdens. The world is full of burdens. And there are the burdens we carry for others—for their well-being, for their spiritual, emotional, and physical health. I have felt it for you, and for many other family members and friends. That's part of loving others; sometimes we carry their burdens.

This is why Jesus bids you and I: come. When you are overwhelmed with the things that have to be done, you can come to Jesus. He understands the pressures of fixing up a broken world. When you are burdened by bills, deadlines, and unrelenting to-do lists, you can come to Jesus. When you are weighed down by the burdens of the world and those you love, you can come to Jesus. He understands. He cares. He lightens our load. He carries eternal peace that He can supernaturally give to us when we are wearied and burdened. I have experienced it often.

Every day when I spend time with God, I talk to Him first about my "to-do list," and I process my negative emotions. I talk to Him about my to-do list because it can burden me and distract me from Jesus. Plus I want Him to be at the center of all I do in life, talking it through with Him is helpful, and I often receive insights from Him as I talk it through. I process my negative emotions because they are often burdensome, and He helps lighten my load and gives me peace. My negative emotions are also often my first indicator that something is "off" in my soul, something is out of alignment with God. So I pay careful attention to those negative emotions because processing them can free me from burdens and help me access Jesus' peace.

Sometimes life feels wearisome because of the sin and evil that has impacted the world. People do things that cause you pain, or say things that hurt your feelings, and you are left feeling wearied and burdened. You feel relational pain, emotional emptiness, and your heart hurts. On top of the personal hurt, sometimes you see the things that are wrong with the world, and you feel the weight and burden of a sin-stricken, evil-marred planet. You want to make a difference, but it is overwhelming because there is so much to do, and it is all so complex to fix. Where do we even begin to make a difference? It's easy to feel burdened and overwhelmed by the pain in the world. The trauma of evil has impacted each of you in different ways, and it leaves all of us with a degree of weariness, emptiness, and heartache. For some of you, the effect of evil in our world leaves you with existential questions. You question the meaning of life. Sometimes it feels like there is no purpose, and it leaves you feeling a bit depressed; sometimes it is even hard to spot hope in the darkness. This is part of the reason why Jesus came. He sees what you see, and He wants you to come with the burden that is too heavy for you to carry. Jesus invites you: come, all you who are weary and burdened.

Whether you are burdened by guilt, shame, condemnation, the never-ending list of things that need to be done, or by the evil in the world, Jesus calls us to come to Him. Come with your burdens; come with your weariness. Come with your emptiness; come with your pain. Come with your hurts; come with your heartaches. Come with your questions; come with your despair. Come as you are. Come to the man of sorrows who is familiar with suffering (Isaiah 53:3), and He will give you rest. He won't answer all your questions, but He will comfort your heart. He won't fix all your problems, but He will calm your fears. He won't fill all your empty places, but He will give you hope. Jesus is never nervous. He is never worn out or weary. He never runs out of compassion or tenderness. Jesus is in Heaven and His soul is at rest, and He can impart His rest to your weary soul. This is what Jesus is like; this is who He is. He cares for all of us when we carry heavy burdens.

The four of you were different ages when I went through that painful season at church when I was under attack from many different directions. I don't know what you remember from those days. I didn't share that much with you at the time because you were young, and I didn't want to burden you, nor did I want it to impact your view of church. The truth is, for the first twelve years of South Shore, it was a beautiful church experience; it was fun and fruitful. And I can honestly say that Jesus did redeem all those difficult years of ministry. I wouldn't change that season for anything in the world. I experienced Jesus' tenderness in the midst of it, His shaping hand because of it, and His redeeming hand on the other side of it. I began to see God's power increase dramatically in my life, and it wouldn't have happened without it.

I wouldn't be who I am without those years. I didn't enjoy going through the latter years, but I can truly say I am glad I did. It changed me. In the midst of pain I often experience the tenderness of Jesus' healing touch. I have grown more in the hard times in life than in the easy times; I have experienced more of Jesus' tenderness in pain than I have in times of peace. I think part of that is simply because I have leaned into Jesus more during the hard times. I have come with my burdens, and He has given me rest. He will do the same for you. But I want you to know that I often had to persist in my coming before I experienced His promised rest. It wasn't always quick or easy; there was a lot of heartache and processing before the peace came. Life is hard, but God is good. And the reality is that life is hard with or without God, but there is much more rest, healing, strength, comfort, and help when I face life's difficulties with God than without Him.

The season of personal attacks went on for about five years. After it ended I had forgiven those who hurt me and thought I was moving forward well. I went to the monastery one day, on a regularly scheduled retreat, and as I drove onto the campus I heard the Lord say, "Mend the nets." It was such an odd expression that I said it out loud to myself, and then I felt anxiety burst in my soul. I went into my room and knelt before the Lord to take my burden to Him. I asked Him what the cause of this sudden burst of anxiety was. Had I sinned? Was it people-pleasing anxiety? Did I have too much going on in my life, and it was a sign of stress? I could not figure out the root. It is always hard to get free from symptoms until we get to the root problem.

I was at the monastery for two and a half days, and the anxiety rippled the entire time. The last day I said to the Lord, "I'm not leaving until you help me with a plan to break this." I heard Jesus say, "Go into the chapel." I went in to wait upon the Lord. I didn't say anything or pray anything; I just waited for Jesus to speak. After some time passed, I heard Jesus say, "Psalm 23." Of course, I know that Psalm well: "The Lord is my shepherd; I shall not want. He makes me lie down in green pastures. He leads me beside quiet waters. He restores my soul." That last phrase grabbed in my spirit. *He restores my soul.* I lingered with it for another half hour or so, and finally the Lord spoke to me: "My presence comes in many forms. There is my healing presence, my loving presence, my empowering presence. But what you need is my restorative presence. You have been on the front lines of the battle. And your soul is tattered and torn. [Thus the phrase: "mend the nets."] The only way to access my restorative presence is through silence and stillness."

Over the next three months, every day I sat before the Lord in silence, and slowly all the anxiety drained away. He healed my soul, picked up my burdens, and restored me to abundant life. This is the Jesus I know! And this is why I love Him.

The picture Jesus uses in this teaching is quite beautiful. He uses the image of a yoke, a double yoke for two oxen to pull together. Much of the time Jesus spoke to people in an agricultural setting. They were used to seeing oxen teamed together, pulling the weight of the plow across the field, and helping one another carry the burden of the work. Farmers often teamed young, strong oxen with older, experienced oxen. As you can imagine, this would allow the older oxen to benefit from the strength of youth, and the younger oxen would benefit from the wisdom of the aging one. Jesus invites us to come under His leadership, and He will pull with us to lift the weight of the burdens of life in a broken world.

You aren't alone, even though you feel lonely sometimes. He is right there with you, wanting to pull the load. He tenderly invites you to come to Him. But we must accept His invitation and choose to come.

I will always be here for you any time you call. I always want you to come to me and be open and honest and vulnerable with me: because I love you, and nothing can change that because you are my kids. I always want to help you, serve you, care for you, and come alongside you to carry the burden, but the reality is that sometimes I cannot be there for you. It may be because I am across the planet at the time of a crisis, or it may be because I am sick. And of course, one day, it will be because I have died and gone to Heaven. But Jesus can always be there for you, and He always cares, more than you or I will ever fully comprehend.

He wants you to know He is no taskmaster. "Take my yoke upon you and learn from me, for I am gentle and humble in heart, and you will find rest for your souls" (Matthew 11:29). When you are weak, He is strong. When you are stubborn,

He is gentle and humble in heart. When you are selfish, He is selfless. When you are confused, He is wise and will lead you. He isn't yelling and telling, pointing the finger of accusation at you. He is picking up the burden, gently and lovingly coaxing you along. He is patiently leading you to the ways of life. There is no one like Jesus. I have walked with Him now for almost forty years, and I haven't just read these words He spoke; I have experienced His soul-strengthening presence throughout my lifetime. I carry more joy, peace, security, confidence, strength, and wholeness in my soul because of my relationship with Jesus than any other factor in life. He has carried me through. Come to Him and He will gently carry you through as well. This is my Jesus; this is the Jesus I know.

> I carry more joy, peace, security, confidence, strength, and wholeness in my soul because of my relationship with Jesus than any other factor in life. He has carried me through.

Do you remember the time we were on vacation in New Hampshire and Danielle cut her foot? We were a long way from the car, and I carried her piggyback out of the woods for much of the way back to the car. Then we drove her to the hospital so she could get stitched up. When you were little, if you fell asleep in the van, I would pick you up and carry you into the house and lay you down in your bed. When you are weary now, I can be an emotional support to you—and I would drop anything to be there for you—but Jesus can carry you in ways no one else can. And when I am gone, He will still be with you. I want you to know I have felt His heavenly arms lifting me in life's darkest hours—whether through relational pain, emotional pain, or ministry pain. I have experienced His rest, and it is as available to you as it has been to me.

## The Peace of Jesus

Jesus goes about His ministry: healing the sick, casting out demons, teaching people about the Kingdom of God, and the people love Him! But a dark cloud begins to rise on the horizon because the religious leaders hate Him. Envy consumes their capacity to see Him for who He is; they were envious because He was winning the hearts of the people. Sadly, if they would have admitted their envy and come to Jesus, He would have forgiven them and helped them get free. It is pride that most often prevents us from admitting that we need help, and then from reaching out for it. Unwilling to humble themselves, these religious leaders began to plot Jesus' death. Jesus knew this was coming, for He knew this was why He had come to earth. Something had to be done to address the problem of evil in the world; something had to be done to overthrow the tyrannical rule of hell. God's solution was that Jesus would come, become one of us, enter the fray with us, be tempted like us but overcome, suffer with us and for us, and God would redeem His death to bring us life. He would take upon Himself sin and all its effects, and He would give us all the benefits of Heaven beginning here on earth. So Jesus, knowing this was what He came to do, began to warn His disciples about His impending death.

You probably remember the story of the first time Jesus told His disciples He would have to die. He had just asked them who people said He was, and they told Him the word on the street was that He was probably some prophet resurrected. Then He asked them who they thought He was. Peter, ever the spokesman for the group, leaned in hard and said, "You are the Messiah, the Son of the living God" (Matthew 16:16). Jesus commended Him for believing this revelation He had received from the Father. But on the heels of this declaration of Jesus' identity, Jesus began to tell the disciples He would die. The first time Peter heard this, he rebuked Jesus—it blew up his worldview of the Messiah, and it was more than he could bear. From that time on, Jesus started talking to them about His death.

There was so much confusion for the disciples over this issue. They had this triumphant view of a conquering hero-Messiah. They didn't have any space for a suffering servant Messiah—even though both views of the Messiah are presented in the Old Testament. But Jesus persisted in telling them, and they started feeling the weight of His imminent death. One day Jesus is talking to them about this, and He predicts Peter's denial. There is a heaviness in the room and Jesus seeks to comfort them—even though He is the one about to be betrayed, He is the one about to die. I want to look with you at those words of comfort because they reveal to us, once again, the tender heart of the Savior.

These words are likely familiar to you because they are often read at funerals. But Jesus spoke these words to comfort His disciples concerning His own upcoming crucifixion. Jesus said, "Do not let your hearts be troubled. Trust in God; trust also in me. My Father's house has plenty of room; if that were not so, would I have told you that I am going there to prepare a place for you? And if I go and prepare a place for you, I will come back and take you to be with me that you also may be where I am" (John 14:1-3).

Picture the scene and think about the human aspects of it. It seems to me that sometimes we spiritualize too many things in the church. But Jesus became human so He could bring God into our ordinary lives. Jesus is telling them He is going to die and that they are going to deny Him. The mood is weighty, somber. They are confused; they simply have no frame of reference for this. Jesus sees that they are downcast. Remember, they have left everything behind to follow Jesus, and now it appears all is going to be lost. They are about to lose the One on whom they have put their hope. Jesus is telling them He will rise again in three days, but they can't make sense of His death, much less His resurrection. So, in their minds, they are about to lose their hopes for a better future.

They have been an upstart, entrepreneurial, apostolic movement of Kingdom movers, and now He is telling them that He is going to die and, as far as they can see, the enterprise they have banked on is going to the grave with Him. Of course, He had already told them the church would prevail, but it was hard for them to hold onto that in this dark hour.

Seeing their mood, Jesus offers them tender words of comfort and hope. "Do not let your hearts be troubled. Trust in God; trust also in me" (14:1). Of course, they can't see the way out of death, but Jesus can. Jesus can always see a way out when we have long since given up. The disciples have only ever known death as an end, not as a beginning. They have only experienced death as a cause for grieving, not a reason for celebration. They have only envisioned death as the ultimate defeat, not as the launching pad to victory. One of the great problems with following Jesus is He doesn't think like we do. The Lord said, "For my thoughts are not your thoughts, neither are your ways my ways" (Isaiah 55:8). God saves us by becoming one of us. He redeems us by being tempted like we are and overcoming. He seals the victory through death, then He defeats death through resurrection and ascension. No one would have written the drama like this. We all want the hero to ride into town on his white horse, destroy the enemy, and establish the reign of good over evil—all without any pain and suffering.

Jesus sees their confusion and offers them compassionate understanding. He patiently calls them to trust even though they cannot yet see. He offers them comfort in their current distress even though that distress is the path to their greatest comfort. I love Jesus because He takes the really complex things of God and makes them accessible to us.

> I love Jesus because He takes the really complex things of God and makes them accessible to us.

When you were little, one night I was reading a children's Bible with Danielle. We read the story of Jesus' death on the cross. She was not yet five years old, and she asked me, "Daddy, why did Jesus die on the cross?" This is a complex theological question that people have written about for two thousand years, and I had to explain it to a four-year-old! I said, "Danielle, you know how sometimes you go outside, and you play in the dirt, and you get all dirty? When you come inside, before you eat, you have to wash your hands, right?" You agreed. I said, "Well, when you do something naughty, like you hit your sister or lie to your parents, you get dirt on your heart. How can you wash your heart? Do you have a zipper on your chest?" You looked down to check—just to be sure—then you shook your head and your eyes got wide with curiosity wondering how we were going to solve this problem! I said, "That's why Jesus died on the cross. We can't just unzip our chest and wash our own heart, so Jesus died to wash away all the naughty things we do. We have to ask Him to come into our lives, then He lives in our hearts, and when we do naughty things, He can wash our hearts clean so we can be friends with God." You looked at me with understanding and asked, "Does Jesus live in my heart?" I said, "Did you invite Him to?" You shook your head again. That night you invited Jesus into your heart.

A few days later I had an interesting conversation with Courtney. We were standing on the stairs in the house on Bedford Street in Bridgewater when Courtney asked me, "Do you know where Jesus lives?" She was three years old. I said, "He lives in Heaven." She said, "Do you know where else He lives?" I asked, "Where?" She said, "Inside my heart!" I said, "How did He get in there?" I was curious! Courtney said, "You know when you go outside, and you get dirty? What do you have to do before you eat dinner?" I said, "Wash my hands." She said, "You know when you do something naughty—like yell at me—your heart gets dirty. Do you have a zipper on your chest?" I looked down just to check! I said, "Nope." She said, "So, how can you clean your heart? That's why Jesus came and died on the cross. If you invite Him into your heart, then He can make your heart clean so you can be friends with God."

Danielle, you had taken what I said to you, and told Courtney, and Courtney turned around and relayed that right back to me. I was ready to invite Jesus into my heart right then and there! I had explained the death of Jesus, which provides for our forgiveness, to a four-year-old so that she not only understood it but was able to communicate it to a three-year-old so she could understand it and communicate it to others. Jesus takes the complexities of Heaven and makes them understandable to people like us. Jesus takes the transcendent immensity of God and makes Him relatable to mortals like us.

We have so many questions. There is so much we do not understand. This world is broken, dark, difficult, painful, and we want to comprehend it. Jesus explains things to us, He shows us the way, and when it is all still too much for us, He offers us His loving presence and tender words of comfort. I said it before: there are a lot of things in this world that I do not understand. I do not understand why things happen the way they happen, but I know I can trust God because of the cross. This is the ultimate proof that God is with us and God is for us. This is the irrefutable evidence that God cares. And here, in John 14, on the brink of His own departure, Jesus offers His grieving disciples words of hope. He is saying to them, "I know you do not understand why this is happening. I know the thought that I am going to die is greatly troubling to you. I know it is contrary to your every way of thinking. But you can trust your good Father, and you can trust Me."

This is often the way in my relationship with God. I remember the first time Mom and I hit a marriage snag. At the time only Danielle and Courtney were around, and Courtney was a baby. We were working hard to repair our relationship; every night we were embroiled in difficult, trouble-shooting conversations, and it often felt like we were getting nowhere. One day I was praying about it, and I had this inner sense that God was speaking to me again, and He said, "I want you to thank me for this marriage struggle." One of the reasons I'm convinced this was God saying this to me is because I never would have had that thought on my own, and it is consistent with what God says elsewhere in Scripture.

I said to the Lord, "I am grateful for many things, but this marriage crisis is not on the list." I sensed the Lord saying, "One day, you will be more grateful for this than just about anything that comes into your life. Today, give me thanks for it in faith. I will redeem it." So I did what was utterly contrary to my way of thinking. I thanked God for the marriage pain. And look how God has redeemed it. Out of that crisis came *Soul Care,* and that book and the resulting conferences have literally helped hundreds of thousands of people around the world find freedom. Now I can easily see how God has redeemed it. But it doesn't take faith to believe God after He has redeemed it, when the results have come in. It surely takes faith to believe God when we are in the darkness. Will we trust Him then? Jesus' tenderness, compassion, love, life, and death are the proof that we can trust God even in the darkest hour.

Jesus is inviting His disciples, and us, to trust Him in the difficult times, in the darkest hour. We will never develop into people of spiritual depth if we don't learn how to trust God and allow Him to redeem the dark times in our life. This has been one of my greatest battles, and one of my greatest victories. I have come to the place where I have gotten better at trusting God in the darkest hour. I certainly haven't perfected it; my faith has often been wobbly. But I am learning. Every time suffering comes into my life, I pick up Romans 8:28-39 and James 1:2-5 and I claim the promises there. God promises us He can redeem everything that comes into our life to make us more like Jesus. It isn't that everything is good; it is that God is so good that, even when evil touches us, if He touches the evil, He can make good from it. James agrees with Paul's thinking in Romans 8, and he tells us that we can rejoice in trials because God can redeem them to make us whole, complete, lacking nothing. James goes on to say that if we lack wisdom when we are going through a trial, and we don't know how God can redeem it to make us mature, we should ask Him, and He will give us wisdom. So every time I suffer, I take these promises and I pray them back to God. I say, "Lord, you promised you would redeem this in my life to make me know and become more like Jesus. Show me how. Show me what you are doing in me, and I will cooperate." In the face of suffering, I have stopped asking God, "Why?" And I started asking him, "How? How can you redeem this?" That has made a huge difference in my trusting God in the dark times.

I hope you don't think I am saying this means everything will work out the way you hope and plan. It surely will not. The disciples hoped in this situation that Jesus wouldn't die, but that He would put Israel back on the map as a self-governed nation. Jesus didn't fulfill their wishes, but He did redirect their attention and do more than they could imagine. The message of Jesus is the good news about the Kingdom of God, and the Kingdom of God is eternal, not temporal. It is manifest in our temporal world—through reconciliation with God, healings, deliverances, life change, encounters with God, justice, freedom, and in many other ways that reverse the effects of sin and evil. But its ultimate and final fulfillment cannot occur outside of eternity. That's the nature of the Kingdom of God.

So Jesus brings His disciples back to the eternal focus. He told them, "My Father's house has plenty of room; if that were not so, would I have told you that I am going there to prepare a place for you? And if I go and prepare a place for you, I will come back and take you to be with me that you also may be where I am" (John 14:2, 3). Listen: there is room in the Father's house for all. Jesus' invitation is for all. Peter wrote that God wishes that none should perish—not one person should miss out on the abundant life that Jesus offers (2 Peter 3:9). Heaven is a big place, God has a big heart, and there is plenty of room in Heaven and the heart of God for anyone who wants to join God's family. No matter what they have done, no matter what has been done to them, no matter what side of the tracks they grew up on, no matter the color of their skin, no matter their economic status, no matter their political persuasion. There is room in God's heart and God's house for all. Jesus' arms are open wide, and His invite is tenderly offered to any who will receive Him. Jesus is the most radically inclusive person who ever lived.

> Jesus' arms are open wide, and His invite is tenderly offered to any who will receive Him. Jesus is the most radically inclusive person who ever lived.

I cannot make sense of this sin-scarred world without factoring in eternity. Not every problem on earth will be solved; not every injustice on earth will be overturned. Not every sick person on earth will be healed; not every oppressed person will be free. Not every evildoer on earth will be caught and pay for their crimes; not every broken person will be restored. This side of Heaven, life doesn't always work the way it should, and good doesn't always triumph over evil. Heaven will resolve all of earth's problems and fulfill all of God's promises.

Jesus' promise to those early disciples, and to us, is that He will take us to be where He is so we can be with Him. Heaven will be a place where there is no more sickness, death, evil, temptation, sin, darkness, depression, unfulfilled longings, heartaches, injustices, oppression, or suffering. Paul said, "For now we see only a reflection as in a mirror; then we shall see face to face. Now I know in part; then I shall know fully, even as I am fully known" (1 Corinthians 13:12). We are looking at God and life through a distorted lens, but Heaven will clear up all distortions, and we will see clearly. When you are with Jesus, you will see Him clearly in all His beauty, all His perfection, all His tender love.

I wish I could convey to you more clearly what is in my heart. I cannot tell you how often I write these words to you on the verge of tears—tears because of my love for Jesus and my love for you. And tears because of Jesus' love for you, which I long for you to know and experience in ever deepening ways. Paul got it. I love the following description of Jesus' love in Paul's letter to the Romans. It is right after the passage where He says God can redeem everything that comes into our lives to make us more like Jesus. He goes on to write: "What, then, shall we say in response to these things? If God is for us, who can be against us? He who did not spare his own Son, but gave him up for us all—how will he not also, along with him, graciously give us all things? Who will bring any charge against those whom God has chosen? It is God who justifies. Who then can condemn? No one. Christ Jesus who died—more than that, who was raised to life—is at the right hand of God and is also interceding for us. Who shall separate us from the love of Christ? Shall trouble or hardship or persecution or famine or nakedness or danger or sword? . . . No, in all these things we are more than conquerors through him who loved us. For I am convinced that neither death nor life, neither angels nor demons, neither the present nor the future, nor any powers, neither height nor depth, nor anything else in all creation, will be able to separate us from the love of God that is in Christ Jesus our Lord" (Romans 8:31-39).

Danielle, Courtney, Darcy, Craig—and you too, dear reader—that is how you are loved. Read it slowly; read it aloud. Put your name in the passage because Jesus loves you like this, and He proved it with His life and death on a cross. God is for you. God did not spare His Son for you. God gave Him up for you. God will let no charge stand against you. Jesus intercedes for you. Jesus died for you. Nothing can remove Jesus' love from you. No matter how hard life gets, Jesus is for you, Jesus is with you, and Jesus loves you with all the tender affections of eternal love!

### Experience

Take time to sit with Jesus once more and simply be still. The world is full of bad news, but Jesus' message is good news. He comes to offer the weary soul help on the journey, a lighter load. He promises peace to those who are troubled by the trials and circumstances of life. Come to Jesus today with your bad news, your angst, your wearisome troubles and trials, and give them to Him. You may find it helpful to picture Jesus sitting with you, across the table from you, or next to you on the couch, and simply hand him your trials. Let the Holy Spirit guide you, speak to you, and minister Jesus' life-giving, load-bearing presence to you. Watch and listen. Rest and receive.

*"There is no sweeter fellowship with Christ than to bring our wounds and our sores to Him."*

– SAMUEL RUTHERFORD[4]

Four
___

# TENDERNESS IN DEATH

There is no greater display of the loving tenderness of Jesus than His death on the cross. The week that He died, Jesus said to His disciples, "Greater love has no one than this: to lay down one's life for one's friends" (John 15:13). I have walked with Jesus for many years, and I am still so deeply moved by the incredible story of Jesus' life on earth that led to His death for us. It leaves us with the most bewildering question: Why? Why did God become a man and die for us? The only explanation is His great love.

One of the reasons I am a Christian is because the Christian worldview makes sense. It is not hard to see the impact of sin and evil on the world—injustice, war, oppression, racism, hatred, violence, abuse, rape, murder, addiction, selfishness, and every evil known to humanity. It is always easy to compare ourselves to people worse than us and think we are doing well. But the reality is that it isn't just the world that has been impacted by sin and evil; you and I have sinned too. I have said careless words that have hurt you and others I love. At times I have been selfish, insensitive, inconsiderate, proud, rude, and hurtful. I have violated the most basic rule of all, the rule of love. It was my selfishness that led to that breakup story I told at the beginning, and it was, in part, my selfishness that led Mom and I to our first marriage crisis. She too contributed to the relational hurt and pain. Fortunately, I have grown and changed, and I am a much better human than I used to be. But I still sin and hurt people I love.

Jesus said the most important thing is to love God and love people, and I have not done this perfectly, even on my best day. He said that we should treat others the way we want to be treated (the Golden Rule), but I have often fallen short. The problem with the world is not just that it is stained by sin; the problem with the world is that every person who exists is stained by sin. I contribute to the brokenness of the world. So what do we do with the reality of sin? Every major religion agrees that the problem with humanity is sin. Where these religions differ is what to do with that reality. Most simply prescribe some sort of pick-yourself-up-by-the-bootstraps self-improvement philosophy. But that neither gets rid of my propensity to make life too much about me, nor does it rid my soul of the stain of my sin. So what then?

Biblical Christianity says Jesus loved us too much to leave the barrier of sin between us and God; He loved too greatly to leave this world in its troubled state of sin-saturated brokenness. So He intervened. Jesus came and did what had to be done in the name of love, for the sake of love. The cross is God's

The cross is God's answer to sin. The cross is God's love letter to a rebellious world. The cross is the hope of Heaven.

answer to sin. The cross is God's love letter to a rebellious world. The cross is the hope of Heaven. The cross is the path back to God and wholeness.

If the cross is true, as the Bible claims, it is clearly the most important story in human history. So let's take a closer look at some of the snapshots of this compelling story.

On the night Jesus was betrayed, He ate the Passover with His disciples. The Passover was a feast celebrating the time when Israel miraculously escaped from slavery in Egypt through the plagues God sent on a proud and oppressive king and his nation who would not humble themselves. The final plague was the death of the firstborn. The Israelites smeared the blood of a lamb on their doorposts to escape the angel of death. On every door where the angel saw the blood, he passed over that house. Why was this necessary?

If you remember, when God created Adam and Eve, He set them in a beautiful garden and told them they could have dominion over the earth and eat anything they wanted. There was only one thing forbidden: they could not eat the fruit from the knowledge of the tree of good and evil. If they ate this fruit, God told them, they would die. Of course they ate it, and sin, death, and evil entered the human race. This is known as the fall of humanity: with this fall came the human propensity to go our own way, to make life too much about us, to reject God, to make our own standards of right and wrong, and to violate God's standards and do evil. As I said earlier, the real issue is not the sins we commit, but the fact that we are sinners. We push God out of the center of our lives and rebel against Him by going our own way, doing our own thing. God had to deal with more than our behavior; He had to deal with the condition of our hearts. We reject God and God's Golden Rule of putting others first in love, and we choose the rule of self: I do what is best for me. I am never concerned that you sin; everyone sins, and we will keep on sinning until we die. I am only concerned when you don't put Jesus at the center of your life. When Jesus is at the center, He will lead us out of bad behaviors and into good ones. When Jesus is at the center of your life, life will be the best it can be in a broken world. When Jesus isn't at the center, even if you do a lot of good things, at best you will only become like a Pharisee. We can't clean our own hearts.

Despite Adam and Eve's rebellion, God persisted in loving them and wanting a relationship with them. So God, because of His love for His creation, created a path to redeem them, the first man and woman, to rescue them from the clutches of the enemy of our souls. What could He do with sin and death? If He ignored it, He would not continue to be good or just. Imagine you had children of your own and someone abused them, yet the man who did it was completely unrepentant. He was brought before a judge in a trial, and the judge dismissed the case. He said, "While he did these horrible things to your children, he has helped old ladies cross the street and he has given money to the poor." "Yes, but he abused children!" you would argue. "Are you just going to ignore that?" Do we want a judge who ignores evil acts? Not if it is your life or your child you don't!

The payment for sin is death. So someone had to pay the debt of sin so justice could be served. In the Old Testament the Hebrews sacrificed animals—God allowed them to substitute the death of an animal in exchange for their life. It was to remind them of the weightiness of sin. The stakes were life and death. So, on the Passover, they sacrificed the Passover Lamb. The people realized that someone had to pay for their sins; there is no forgiveness of sins without the shedding of blood (Hebrews 9:22). But the blood of the Passover Lamb was merely a foreshadowing of what had to happen because the blood of animals could not make up for the sin of humans.

When John the Baptist started preaching, he said, "Look, the Lamb of God, who takes away the sin of the world!" (John 1:29) Jesus died on Passover week because He was the true Passover Lamb. He was the One who died so we could live. He was the Lamb of God who died to remove the stain of sin from each of our souls. His shed blood allows us to escape the angel of death—this angel "passes over" us. When Jesus ate the Passover with His disciples, He explained that the bread was His body broken for us and the wine His blood shed for the forgiveness of our sins. "Then he took the cup, and when he had given thanks, he gave it to them, saying, 'Drink from it, all of you. This is my blood of the covenant, which is poured out for many for the forgiveness of sins'" (Matthew 26:27, 28).

God created a new covenant with us. You humble yourself and trust Jesus, and He forgives all your wrongdoing, adopts you into His eternal family, and deposits His Holy Spirit in you to do life with you so you are never alone; you can draw near to God, and you can live a victorious life with the help of the Spirit. He welcomes you into Heaven when this life is over, and you will be forever free from the evil effects of sin. It is an amazing story of deep, tender love. One of the problems with growing up in the church is that the story becomes so familiar it can easily lose its wonder. We need fresh revelation from the Holy Spirit to reawaken awe in our souls for what Jesus has done for us.

I had heard this story my entire life. But it didn't make a deep impact on me, and Jesus remained at the edges of my life, until I encountered His love after that breakup. One encounter with Jesus' love changed me forever.

Jesus died because He had to, and Jesus died because He loves you. If there was another way for sin to be forgiven and us to be reconciled to God, He would have chosen it. That night in the Garden of Gethsemane, Jesus agonized over His death. It is one of these beautiful moments in the Gospels where we see Jesus' tender heart—for His Father, and for us.

> Jesus died because He had to, and Jesus died because He loves you.

After the Passover meal, Jesus went to the garden to pray. He brought the disciples with Him, but He allowed Peter, James, and John, His inner circle of three, to come a little farther than the rest. He shared His heart with them in His darkest hour: "My soul is overwhelmed with sorrow to the point of death. Stay here and keep watch with me" (Matthew 26:38). There is a difference between transparency and vulnerability. When we are transparent, we are open, honest, and confessional. But we can be transparent and distant; we can expect nothing in return from the one with whom we share. When we are vulnerable, we are open, honest, and transparent, but we expect something from the other person. We expect them to be there for us, and with us; we entrust ourselves to them in some way, and if they don't come through, we are hurt. Vulnerability exposes us; it opens us to the possibility of heartbreak. This moment was so painful, so intense, for Jesus that He needed some friends to be there with Him and for Him. Sadly, they let Him down.

I think Jesus was overwhelmed with sorrow in this moment for a variety of reasons. First, He was going to die, and every human has an instinct to live. Yet I suspect this was not the reason that weighed heaviest on Jesus. Second, I think Jesus felt the impact of sin on the world more than anyone who ever lived. He was facing the weight of that reality here in the garden. Third, Jesus was about to experience the weight of evil transferred to His account on the cross, and it would cause Him to be separated from His Father. This is the one I think probably pained Him the most. I'd like to go a little deeper with these last two reasons because they show us the heart of Jesus.

Let's talk about the devastating impact of sin on the world. One of the things we need to understand about God is how deeply sin, evil, and pain grieve Him. He hates suffering because He loves people. I think sometimes we are tempted to think God is removed, indifferent, and aloof to human suffering. But if that were true, Jesus wouldn't have come and suffered with us and suffered for us. If that were true, Jesus wouldn't have shed tears and grieved over people's suffering. I haven't covered the story of Lazarus's resurrection (John 11) in this book, but it is a beautiful account. One of the remarkable pieces of that story is that Jesus wept—even though He came to the tomb specifically to raise Lazarus from the dead. He knew, supernaturally, that Lazarus had died, and He knew He would raise him from the dead; He told His disciples both things ahead of time. Yet He still wept. Jesus wept at Lazarus's tomb because He sees what a mess sin has made of the world.

Sin has caused so much pain, suffering, sorrow, and grief, and the pain of life moved Jesus to tears.

As I travel the world doing Soul Care Conferences, I listen to a lot of stories; everyone's story has been impacted by sin and evil. You and I, my four children, are lucky to have grown up in a decent home with loving parents. Even so, we have been hurt. We have hurt you with careless words, unwise parenting, and distracted inattentiveness; you have hurt one another with words and deeds, and other people have hurt us as well. That's the sad reality of sinful choices: they cause pain. But I have to tell you that sometimes I hear a story that is so painful, so tragic, it pierces my heart, and I am moved to tears. This week I was doing a Soul Care Conference and I did another deliverance where someone was sexually abused by her father, and he allowed his friends to abuse her sexually too. It is so evil and vile it is hard to comprehend. I have to tell you, as a dad to you three lovely young ladies, I cannot imagine someone doing this to their daughter, and yet I run into this sort of thing at every Soul Care Conference, and my heart is always stricken with pain for these dear women who should have been deeply loved by their fathers. I always feel Jesus' broken heart for the world. Sometimes I watch how the sin and evil of this world impacts your lives and I am moved to tears. That's why Jesus came, and that's why He agonized in the garden. The tragic results of sin in our world moved Him with tender compassion, and He came to rescue us from the impact of sin. Jesus came to cleanse our sin-stained hearts and heal our wounded souls. Thus, Jesus is so often "moved with compassion" as He heals the sick, casts out demons, cares for the needy, and teaches those who are harassed and helpless like sheep without a shepherd.

In the Garden Jesus feels the weight of human sin and the devastation it has caused. All the evil choices of humanity have led to this inevitable moment in history. All the rape, molestation, violence, murder, anger, abuse, hatred, oppression, prejudice, racism, envy, jealousy, robbery, abuse of power, selfishness, slander, bitterness, and every other form of evil and malice have come to no other conclusion but the cross. All of history, and the entire Old Testament narrative, have been building to this crescendo. Evil could not be ignored, yet God's love could not be denied. Sin could not be overcome without a divine intervention. Listen: I have lived fifty-seven years, and the world has not gotten any better in my lifetime. Sure, some things have improved, but many others have gotten worse. Overall, things are definitely not getting better. People are still people, and they are still doing the things they have always done. No amount of education has changed all the evil deeds of humanity. No matter how much you and I try, we cannot snuff out the fire of evil in our own lives much less the world. From the very beginning of Jesus' public ministry, He knew this would be the end, the fulfillment of His calling. All the sin and evil of the world led Him to the cross.

I think perhaps the biggest reason Jesus felt such overwhelming sorrow in the Garden was that He was going to take our sins upon Himself on the cross, and this would separate Him from His Father. Paul makes a remarkable statement about what Jesus did on the cross. He writes, "God made him who had no sin to be sin for us, so that in him we might become the righteousness of God" (2 Corinthians 5:21). What do you do with the problem of evil in the world? What do you do with the sin that has stained every human heart and harmed every human relationship? What do you do with all our cumulative evil choices and negative consequences? Jesus, who was tempted in every way we are, yet without sin (Hebrews 4:15), became sin for us to bear upon Himself all the tragic consequences of sin. All the sins of humanity were placed upon His perfectly pure and beautiful soul. All the things I have ever done that were selfish, hurtful, wrong, and evil Jesus took up on the cross. Every unloving word, thought, and action were absorbed into Jesus' flawless soul. There was a transference that took place—my sins were transferred to Jesus' account before the Father. He paid for my sin with His blood, and now the blood of Christ marks my soul so that the angel of death will pass over me, and I can experience the eternal life of the Spirit of God within me beginning now and ultimately culminating in Heaven. But, of course, He didn't just do it for me, nor just for you, but for all people. No matter what we have done. No matter how bad we have messed up. That's why we call it Good News.

Jesus felt the weight of what He was about to do that night long ago in a garden. He felt the weight of becoming sin. Imagine being so pure and having all the sins of humanity transferred to your soul. All the sins I have heard confessed at Soul Care Conferences—it is overwhelming for me to think about. I cannot tell you how many times someone has burst into tears in front of me because of the devastating results of their tragic choices. They would do anything to go back and change them, but they cannot. Fathers who have abused their children, wives who have abandoned their husbands for another, addicts who have chosen the bottle over their loved ones—they all carry guilt and pain, and if they could do it over again, they would go back and make better choices. But they cannot. This is why we need forgiveness. You and I may not have sinned in the same way as some of these tragic examples, but no one lives life without causing someone else pain, and when they realize that, if they have any degree of humility, they feel the pain of their poor choices and the longing to be set free from their wrongs. This is why Jesus came.

Forgiving someone always comes at a personal cost. The good news is that you are set free from the bondage of bitterness when you forgive. But there is a price to pay. You are giving up your right to be justified, giving up your desire to defend yourself, releasing your need to set the record straight, forgoing your longing for revenge, taking up someone's wrongdoing only to let it go and release them. There is a death to our self-life, and it is painful to die. When I went through that season of attacks at church, I had to forgive people who spoke ill of me; they never owned their wrongdoing and never apologized. It hurt, and that is the nature of forgiveness. But when I forgave them, I gave up my right to rehearse the offense or nurse grudges. I released them from my heart without ever receiving an apology or any repayment for the damage done. But I am not completely innocent in any relationship, and no doubt some of their anger was directed at me because of my own wrongs. Jesus, though, never sinned. He never did anything wrong, and all the sin of everyone in the world was transferred to Him. Imagine the weight, the overwhelming ghastly feeling of sorrow, grief, and pain He felt.

What makes this even more painful is that when Jesus became sin, it separated Him from His Father. Jesus cried out

> Forgiving someone always comes at a personal cost. There is a price to pay.

on the cross, "My God, my God, why have you forsaken me?" (Matthew 27:46) Sin separates us from God. Jesus became sin and endured our separation from God so that we might become the righteousness of God and be reconciled to Him. All our sin was washed away that day, but it cost Jesus a break in His eternal connection to His Father. They had never known any separation, and the rejection of His Father in that moment broke His heart. But He became sin so He could take up our rejection. The reason Jesus suffered for us is because He was moved with compassion. Gut-wrenching tenderness drove Him to the cross.

> The reason Jesus suffered for us is because He was moved with compassion. Gut-wrenching tenderness drove Him to the cross.

Jesus prayed in the Garden: "My Father, if it is possible, may this cup be taken from me. Yet not as I will, but as you will" (Matthew 26:39). Jesus felt the weight of His assignment. He felt the heaviness of a world full of evil; He felt the grievous reality of becoming sin and facing separation from the Father. And He asked the Father for a way out, if it was possible, if there could be any other way to accomplish the redemptive purposes of God.

Let's go back to the Garden for a moment. Just a few thoughts about these intense moments for Jesus. First, Jesus prays for a way out, but is completely surrendered: "not as I will, but as you will." Rebellion against God got humanity into the mess of a sin-marred planet, and only surrender to God could lead us out. Jesus understood that and freely surrendered; His loyalty to the Father was unwavering. Second, no other way but the cross comes forth because there is no other way. There was no other way to deal with evil and demonstrate compassion. There was no other way to express God's goodness, justice, and mercy in the face of treacherous wrongdoing. There was no other way for God to convince us of His tenderness in the face of suffering except to suffer with us and for us on the cross. So Jesus came. Third, the cup that Jesus drinks is the cup of suffering. He drinks of the cup of suffering for a world infected by, and suffering under, sin so that we can be cleansed. He drinks of the cup of our corporate suffering, our personal suffering, the suffering we have experienced, and the suffering we have caused others. He drinks of the cup of our suffering and His suffering. Mingling our tears with His tenderness, Jesus provides the only way out of sin and suffering on the cross.

Sadly, when Jesus returns to them, His entrusted traveling companions have fallen asleep. "Couldn't you men keep watch with me for one hour? Watch and pray so that you will not fall into temptation. The spirit is willing, but the flesh is weak" (Matthew 26:40, 41). I have to say, I love the disciples because they are weak, flawed people like us. And they are honest and record their failings for us, and I love them for that. They weren't hiding, pretending, or defending themselves. Authentic humility begins with honesty; it ends with responsibility, and somewhere in the middle is death to self. The disciples are honest about their flaws, weaknesses, and sin; they take responsibility for their lives. One of the benefits of experiencing Jesus' tender love is the security you feel that allows you to humble yourself and be honest; you don't feel the need to hide or be secretive because you discover that you are loved at your very worst, flaws and all. You are loved just as you are. This is incredibly empowering and freeing.

After exhorting the disciples to keep watch so they wouldn't fall away, Jesus goes back to pray again. He shifts His prayer from "if it is possible" to "My Father, if it is not possible for this cup to be taken away unless I drink, may your will be done" (Matthew 26:42). Jesus knew that He had come for this moment, but He was hoping the Father could pave another path forward to rescue humanity. But after His first round of prayer, He was becoming more convinced there was no other path. The truth was He knew this was His assignment from the beginning of His ministry—but the pain of the cross caused Him to hope for some other path forward. It wasn't possible, however, to save a world from suffering and avoid the cup of suffering, nor could Jesus save a world bound by sin without becoming sin for us. The prophet Isaiah described Jesus with this phrase, "He was despised and rejected by men; a man of sorrows, and acquainted with grief" (Isaiah 53:3, ESV). He entered our pain and suffering; He suffered with us, and He suffered for us. He is the Man of Sorrows. There is no pain you have experienced that Jesus did not take to the cross, so He is acquainted with your pain and suffering, your sorrow and grief. Jesus drank this horrid cup of suffering for us with soul-stirring tenderness. Isaiah 53 says that Jesus took up our pain and bore our suffering. All the pain you have suffered in life—rejection, hurt, heartache, depression, physical pain, emotional pain, spiritual pain—Jesus absorbed on the cross so He could help you in your suffering. And so you would forever know that God truly cares.

When Jesus returns from His second prayer time, the disciples are asleep again, but this time He doesn't bother to awaken them. He just goes away and prays once more. Luke tells us that the prayer of Jesus was so intense He actually sweat drops of blood. "And being in anguish, he prayed more earnestly, and his sweat was like drops of blood falling to the ground" (Luke 22:44). This rare and painful situation is a medical condition called *hematidrosis*.

Apparently, Jesus never receives an answer from His Father, and He is now entering into the suffering of silence from Heaven. Every human knows what it is to cry out to God in searing pain and feel as though God is silent. Many of the lament Psalms give voice to this common human malady. I know that you have all felt this at times in your life, children, and so have I. Yet we can rest assured that we are not alone: Jesus experienced the silence of Heaven in His most agonizing moment in the garden. He is the Man of Sorrows; He drank the cup of suffering. No matter what you go through, He understands, and He has tender affections for you. You can always cry out to Jesus in your pain. Jesus' suffering shows me the Father cares for me in my suffering.

We must process grief and pain. In my book *Calm in the Storm*, I wrote: "If we don't process our grief, our trust will be diminished. We can't whitewash pain and heartache with pithy religious phrases or a memorized verse of the Bible. This is what a religious person does—they take a truth and put it on like an outer garment, but they fail to internalize it in their inner being so that it becomes part of their life. They have the right words, but religion is skin-deep. Religious people often fail to internalize eternal truths and they face life with a thin soul. True trust is developed when hardships are authentically processed and the pain-stricken heart comes to restful surrender in the eternal arms of the Man of Sorrows" (Rob Reimer, *Calm in the Storm*, pp.64, 65).

Life is painful, but understanding and experiencing the tenderness of Jesus helps heal the brokenhearted. The fact that Jesus entered our human condition and experienced the pain of life in a fallen world assures us that God cares. The cross anchors us to the goodness of God. We know beyond a doubt that God is good because of the cross. We do not understand why everything happens in life, why God does what He does, why God allows what He allows, but we know He is good because of the cross. He didn't stand outside of human pain and suffering with pitiless indifference; He became the Man of Sorrows fully immersed in our brokenness. He surrendered to this assignment because of His tenderness for you and me. He suffered in silence so that when we suffer in silence, we can look to the cross to know we are not alone. Jesus sees, Jesus cares, Jesus understands.

> The cross anchors us to the goodness of God. We know beyond a doubt that God is good because of the cross.

After Jesus finishes praying the third time, Judas shows up with a band of soldiers. Judas betrays Jesus with a kiss. I have always been struck by Jesus' response: "Friend, do what you came for" (Matthew 26:50). "Friend," Jesus says. Judas has been with Jesus for three years, and now he is handing Jesus over to the authorities to be tried and killed. He was there for all of it: Judas heard Jesus' teaching, saw Jesus' miracles, watched Jesus walk on water, experienced the beauty of Jesus' presence for three years, and yet Judas rejected Him after all of that. Yet Jesus, ever tender, never weak, calls Judas His friend, and with courage proceeds do what He came to do. He has no judgment, no condemnation, no hatred to offer anyone. He came to save, not condemn; He came to forgive, not judge.

In the middle of that dark season at church, the Lord said to me one day, "These people are not your enemies; they are duped by your enemy. Your battle is not against flesh and blood." That helped me to humanize, not villainize, the people who were against me.

Forgiveness is a powerful thing. There were a couple of people who led the attacks against me. I learned long ago in my relationship with Jesus to forgive those who hurt me and to bless those who curse me. So I was praying blessings for them every day, and I refused to retaliate or defend myself. I was working through my hurt with God and forgiving them for what they had done. If you do what God tells you to do, God will do what you cannot do—He will change your heart. So I kept blessing, and God did what only God can do, and He changed my heart. He released me from anger and bitterness.

One day one of my staff members was alone with me and asked, "When you think about these people who led the attacks against you, what do you think of them, really?" I burst into tears, and I said, "I love them." He looked at me and said, "That's not human." He was right; it's not. This is the beauty of following Jesus; He empowers you to do things you cannot do on your own. He empowers you to live a supernatural life. Not only does Jesus forgive you for the things you did, He empowers you to become a person you were not able to become. He helps you love when the only natural human response is to hate. Do you see? This is why I love Jesus so much.

Jesus said, "You have heard that it was said, 'Love your neighbors and hate your enemy.' But I tell you, love your enemies and pray for those who persecute you, that you may be children of your Father in heaven. He causes his sun to rise on the evil and the good, and sends rain on the righteous and the unrighteous. If you love those who love you, what reward will you get? Are not even the tax collectors doing that? And if you greet only your own people, what more are you doing than others? Do not even pagans do that?" (Matthew 5:43-47) The single greatest mark that we have been infected with divine love is our capacity to love our enemies. Even the pagans love their friends; we get no credit for that. That's just normal human behavior. But to love our enemies is truly the mark of the divine—this is what Jesus was all about. This is what happens to people who have truly experienced the tenderness of Jesus. They don't just know about it, they haven't just read about it, they didn't just memorize verses about it.

When we experience the tenderness of Jesus, we have tenderness even for those who have hurt us. Loving our enemies is the result of the powerful effect of the cross on a heart that is yielded to Jesus. There is great potential for life change, but it only occurs if we say yes to Jesus and put Him at the center of our life and decision-making. When we say yes to Jesus, He helps us live a life we cannot live on our own. Saying yes to Jesus isn't always easy, or natural, because God's ways do not always make sense to us. But I have discovered that when I trust Him and submit myself to go in God's ways, life works out better. His ways are wiser; He doesn't show us paths to oppress us. He shows us His paths because He loves us and wants our best, and He knows the best paths for us. But it takes trust to choose God's ways over our ways. We have to trust God is good and that He wants our best. This is why we have to know the tenderness of Jesus.

Peter, as we mentioned before, thinks the Kingdom of Jesus is going to be a political rulership, so he grabs a sword and takes a swipe at one of the people in the crowd (who were armed with swords and clubs, according to Matthew 22:47). Fortunately, Peter is more of a fisherman than a swordsman, and he only manages to lop off the man's ear in a "whoops, I missed" moment. And in yet another magnanimous display of tenderness, Jesus heals the man who came to arrest Him (Luke 22:51). Listen: He didn't have to heal the guy. He could have just told His followers to put away their swords. But this is the heart of Jesus: even someone coming armed to lead Him to His death would be treated with gentle, healing care. Jesus isn't just gentle with those who love Him; Jesus is gentle to anyone who is near Him. This is my Jesus, and this is why I love Him so. He has a beautiful soul. Did you know John's gospel tells us the name of the man who had his ear removed is Malchus? I suspect the reason John knew Malchus's name is because later Malchus became a Jesus-follower. That's the power of encountering the tenderness of Jesus: it is irresistible.

You can resist logic, doctrine, good teaching, and well-reasoned arguments. But to experience the tenderness of Jesus firsthand is a compelling, irresistible, life-altering event. And that is what I pray for you, dear children. You could know about it and remain unchanged, but when you experience it, your heart is forever captured. Do all you can to position yourself to receive His tender love. You'll never regret it, and it will change your heart. It is this revelatory experience of Jesus' tender mercy that has made me say yes to Jesus wherever He leads me, no matter what it costs me.

That dark season of attacks started for me because I sensed the Lord calling me to preach revival until it comes. I committed to do whatever Jesus wanted me to do—that is what it means to put Him at the center of life. And I believe it is the secret to success. But I didn't expect that choice to result in so much animosity. When it started, I went to Jesus and simply asked, "Am I doing the right thing? I am just trying to follow you. You told me to preach revival until it comes. Am I doing the right thing?" I heard the Lord say, "Put your hand to the plow and do not look back." That is a biblical expression, and so I kept preaching revival. And the attacks kept coming. Every day I struggled with doubt, and every day I kept asking, "Am I doing the right thing?" And the Lord kept saying one thing: "Put your hand to the plow and do not look back." So I kept preaching despite the pain and the fact I was afflicted with doubts.

One day a woman approached me at church; she was a visitor. She said, "While you were up there speaking today, I saw a vision of you. You were standing behind an old hand plow and you were plowing an old New England field. It was full of rocks and thorns and roots. You were plowing and the plow would fall over. You were sweaty and grimy and weary, but you would not quit." Put your hand to the plow and do not look back. For the next year I kept preaching and kept getting attacked, and one day I was leading a Soul Care Conference and a man I had never met before came up to me and said, "I had a vision of you while you were speaking. You were plowing in a field with an old hand plow. The field was full of rocks and thorns and roots, and the plow kept falling over. You were weary and sweaty and worn out, but you would not quit." Put your hand to the plow and do not look back.

Once again in my life, Jesus was displaying His tenderness by giving me these two people with the same vision and the same words that He had been speaking to me. I was afflicted with self-doubt and pain, and Jesus was displaying His tenderness to me and assuring me that He was pleased with me. This is the Jesus I know. And this is why I am committed to do whatever Jesus tells me to do. That season was so transformational for me. It was only after that long season of suffering that I saw the power of God released in my life in a remarkable way. Following Jesus is not easy in a fallen world, but it is always worth it. And His tender love is always there, strengthening you to follow when the path seems too steep and the obstacles too great to overcome.

> Following Jesus is not easy in a fallen world, but it is always worth it. And His tender love is always there.

The religious leaders took Jesus through a sham trial. They, of course, had already made up their minds. They interrogated Him with questions designed to make Him incriminate Himself, but nothing stuck because He had done nothing wrong. In the end, they indicted Jesus for blasphemy. They asked Him, "'Tell us if you are the Messiah, the Son of God.' 'You have said so,' Jesus replied. 'But I say to all of you: From now on you will see the Son of Man sitting at the right hand of the Mighty One and coming on the clouds of heaven'" (Matthew 26:63, 64). In a dramatic show of incredulity, the high priest tore his clothes and declared that Jesus had committed blasphemy—which was only true if what Jesus said was false. The Jews could not put Him to death, so they took Him before a Roman ruler named Pilate under the capital punishment charge of insurrection.

Through most of Jesus' trials before the Sanhedrin (the ruling Jewish body) and Pilate, He remained silent. Isaiah the prophet had predicted Jesus' death, resurrection, and this silent response. Isaiah 53:7: "He was led like a lamb to the slaughter, and as a sheep before its shearers is silent, so he did not open his mouth." When Jesus told His disciples to put away their swords, He also said to them, "Do you think I cannot call on my Father, and he will at once put at my disposal more than twelve legions of angels? But how then would the Scriptures be fulfilled that say it must happen in this way?" (Matthew 26:53, 54) Jesus' restraint was not because He was powerless to act, but because He was submitting to the Father's will and fulfilling His redemptive purpose. Jesus restrained His power to demonstrate God's tenderness. It takes more self-restraining power to do nothing in the face of attacks than it does to retaliate. It takes more self-restraint to turn the other cheek than it does to counterattack. Submitting Himself to persecution, suffering, humiliation, and death on a cross is the ultimate proof of the gentleness of God. His heart longs to woo us into relationship, not to force us, nor to dominate us. Behold! The Lamb of God who came to take away the sin of the world!

It must have been such a confusing time for the disciples. Again, let's try to see this event through their eyes. As they were coming to Jerusalem earlier that week the throngs of people were hailing Jesus as the coming King. They were riding the triumphant wave, and even though Jesus had told them He was going into Jerusalem to die, they didn't register it. In fairness, He did speak a great deal in parables, and I think they were often confused as to what He was really trying to say to them. They were looking for a deeper meaning. And indeed, there was a much deeper meaning in His death than they could have imagined. But the prediction of His death was not metaphorical. As Judas came and betrayed Him, after the brief skirmish, they took Jesus away to His mock trial while the disciples hung around and watched from a distance.

Jesus had told them that they would all deny Him, of course. Peter, always the first one to speak, denied it fervently, saying he was willing to die for Jesus. Jesus told him, "Peter, before the rooster crows today, you will deny three times that you know me" (Luke 22:34). Sadly, it happened just as Jesus said. The third time, when Peter denied Jesus, the rooster crowed. What a shocking alarm must have gone off in Peter's soul as he heard that rooster crow and couldn't help but recall Jesus' words to him. Luke tells us it wasn't just the crow that rattled Peter. Just at that moment when he denied Jesus and the rooster crowed, "The Lord turned and looked straight at Peter. Then Peter remembered the word the Lord had spoken to him: 'Before the rooster crows today, you will disown me three times.' And he went outside and wept bitterly" (Luke 22:61, 62).

I suppose some people assume that the look Jesus gave Peter was shaming or condemning, but that wouldn't be consistent with the character of Jesus. As we have seen, John wrote that Jesus did not come into the world to condemn the world (John 3:17). There are others who likely think Jesus directed toward Peter a disappointed look. But again, I doubt it, because Jesus had already predicted this would happen. He wasn't surprised. I don't think it was an "I told you so" look, either. I think it was likely a mixture of sadness and compassion. Jesus was saddened by Peter's denials. I am sure it was hurtful to Him. But He was equally sad that Peter had failed and now was crushed by the weight of his own failure. Remember that when Jesus predicted Peter would deny Him, he also said this: "Simon, Simon, Satan has asked to sift all of you as wheat. But I have prayed for you, Simon, that your faith may not fail. And when you have turned back, strengthen your brothers" (Luke 22:31, 32). And once again, even in the midst of His own pain, sorrow, and grief, the tenderness of Jesus is on display for all to see. He is praying for Simon Peter, praying that his faith will not fail, and that when he does return, he will strengthen the others who are weak. Peter falls, but does get up; he stumbles, but he does not lose his faith. He does indeed return and, in the end, he finishes well and even dies for Jesus. And, of course, Peter's failure and Jesus' tenderness to him is hope for all of us—because we all fail Jesus over and over. Jesus' merciful tenderness is greater than all our sin.

> Jesus' merciful tenderness is greater than all our sin.

Jesus has tenderness for us when life is painful and hard, and when we stumble and fall. Jesus has this same gentle compassion for us when we make life hard on ourselves because of our poor choices. He doesn't judge, scorn, or condemn. He simply loves and longs for us to return to Him, and He receives us with open arms. Again, this is why my heart is so completely enamored with Jesus and why I never get away from reading the Gospels.

Pilate tried to set Jesus free for a little while because he knew it was out of envy that the Jewish leaders handed Jesus over (Matthew 27:18). Plus, Pilate's wife had a disturbing dream about Jesus and sent Pilate a note saying that he should have nothing to do with an innocent man (Matthew 27:19). Though he tried to release Jesus, the religious leaders riled up the crowds and had them shout, "Crucify him!" Eventually, Pilate yielded to their wishes.

Jesus was led away to be crucified, but not before He was severely beaten—this was due to the fact that He was charged with insurrection, which led to the worst kinds of punishment. The soldiers "stripped him and put a scarlet robe on him and they twisted together a crown of thorns and set it on his head. They put a staff in his right hand as a scepter. Then they knelt in front of him and mocked him. 'Hail, king of the Jews!' they said. They spit on him and took the staff and struck him on the head again and again. After they had mocked him, they took off the robe and put his own clothes on him. Then they led him away to crucify him" (Matthew 27:28-31). So sad. It is sad what we do to each other as humans. It is sadder still to think that God became one of us, dwelt among us, demonstrated nothing but loving kindness to us, and this is what we did to Him. Of course, Jesus didn't have to do this; He didn't have to subject Himself to this kind of torment. To think that only thirty-three years earlier Jesus was sitting on a celestial throne in Heaven and the angels gathered around Him and worshiped and adored Him. The saints who have died and gone before us gathered around His throne to hail Him as Heaven's eternal King. Now Jesus suffers ignominy and shame on His way to save the people who reject and despise Him. Do you see why I am so taken with Jesus? Who would do that? Who else would possibly live like this? There is no one like Jesus. I have to confess that often, as I have been writing this book for you, I can feel the heat build up in the back of my eyes and a tear slide down my cheek because I am so deeply moved by this heavenly King with unstoppable power who chose to display irresistible tenderness to people like you and me. I want you, and everyone else, to be captured by the love of Christ as I have been. It brings such deep meaning to life on this temporal globe.

They led Jesus to a place called Golgotha making Him carry His own cross until He was too weak to do so anymore. They recruited a man named Simon to carry Jesus' cross for the last leg of the journey (Matthew 27:32). A sign was hung over him: "This is Jesus, the King of the Jews." If only the people really knew who hung there that day.

While Jesus was on the cross, He had some unfinished business to complete. First, His earthly father, Joseph, had long ago died, and He wanted to make sure His mother, Mary, was cared for, so He gave this responsibility to John. "Near the cross of Jesus stood his mother, his mother's sister, Mary the wife of Clopas, and Mary Magdalene. When Jesus saw his mother there, and the disciple whom he loved standing nearby, he said to her, 'Woman, here is your son,' and to the disciple, 'Here is your mother.' From that time on, this disciple took her into his home" (John 19:25-27). It's a beautiful little side story that points us to the caring heart of Jesus. Wanting to leave no business unfinished, He made sure His mother would be cared for. He was carrying the weight of the world's sin on His pure soul, and He had time to make provision for His mother's future.

The second bit of unfinished business arose because Jesus was not crucified alone. There were two thieves crucified on either side of Him. In the beginning, apparently, both mocked Jesus (Matthew 27:44). But for one of the thieves, something shifted as they hung on their crosses together. He watched Jesus' demeanor. He heard Jesus say of His persecutors, "Father, forgive them, for they do not know what they are doing" (Luke 23:34). He saw the sign: "This is Jesus, the King of the Jews." And somehow or other, with the help of the Spirit, he put it together. Finally, he spoke up. As his fellow criminal continued taunting Jesus—"Aren't you the Messiah? Save yourself and us!" (Luke 23:39)—the second one rebuked him. "'Don't you fear God,' he said, 'since you are under the same sentence? We are punished justly, for we are getting what our deeds deserve. But this man has done nothing wrong'" (Luke 23:40, 41).

In his short speech this rebel released some great theology: don't you fear God, since you are under the same sentence? We are under the same sentence before God, but Jesus took up our cause, took up our death sentence, so we could go free, we could be forgiven, we could be reconciled and united to God. But if we refuse Jesus' love, we miss out on our acquittal and are left carrying the weight of our sentence.

In the end, the prisoner turned to Jesus with a heartfelt plea. "'Jesus, remember me when you come into your kingdom.' Jesus answered him, 'Truly I tell you, today you will be with me in paradise'" (Luke 23:42, 43). None of us gets to paradise or God's Kingdom because of our moral achievements or spiritual pedigree. I've served God my entire adult life, but I have not done enough to pay for my sins, stop my sinning, or earn God's forgiveness. Not one of us has an entitled claim to forgiveness or friendship with God. Forgiveness is a gift that is

> God is irresistibly attracted to the contrite of heart, but the proud continue to walk alone.

granted by the offended party; it can never be earned, claimed, or deserved. It can only be humbly received. Authentic humility begins with honest admission of our wrongdoing and our need for God. God is irresistibly attracted to the contrite of heart, but the proud continue to walk alone. That's the one indispensable characteristic of those who draw near to God: they humble themselves. They quit making excuses, and they stop their blaming, arguing, justifying, and denying of their wrongdoing and their need for God. Instead, they humble themselves and make a simple plea to Jesus, the Tender One. It's a plea of hope, a cry for help, a declaration of dependence.

These two things completed, Jesus needed to finish what He came to do: atone for the sins of the world and overthrow the reign of evil and Satan. "Later, knowing that everything had now been finished, and so that the Scripture would be fulfilled, Jesus said, 'I am thirsty.' A jar of vinegar was there, so they soaked a sponge in it, put the sponge on a stalk of the hyssop plant, and lifted it to Jesus' lips. When he had received the drink, Jesus said, 'It is finished'" (John 19:28-30). He had completed His assignment. He had fulfilled the Scripture and the purpose for which He had come. He overcame temptation and the Tempter. He obeyed His Father in the full, without fail. Jesus had become sin for us, taking up the sins of the world, and paying the price for our sin. Jesus died so that we could live; because He triumphed over sin, death would not be able to hold Him down. Jesus took the keys of the Kingdom back by overcoming sin and Satan. Now He could pass the keys back to humanity and, through the empowerment of the Holy Spirit's presence in us, He could leave the mission to us. It is finished. And that left only one thing to do.

The final piece of unfinished work was to give up the ghost, as the old-timers used to say. It was time for Jesus to exit this world and return to His Father. The fight was over. His assignment was completed, and it was time for Him to do what He came to do and give up His life. And He did it with an obedient, surrendered heart, trusting His Father to the very last. "Jesus called out with a loud voice, 'Father, into your hands I commit my spirit.' When he had said this, he breathed his last" (Luke 23:46).

Jesus trusted His Father and only did what the Father told Him to do. He trusted His Father because of His rock-solid belief in the Father's goodness. Jesus came to re-present the Father to us. Our grip on God's goodness has been shaken by sin and the problem of evil in the world. It is Jesus who shows us what God is like and that He is good and completely trustworthy. I trust God because I have experienced the tenderness of Jesus and He has shown me how good and trustworthy His Father is. The cross is the final proof of the ultimate goodness of God.

Before I close this chapter, there is one last, somewhat obscure passage I want to mention. It has always fascinated me. It happened when Jesus died and gave up his spirit. "At that moment the curtain of the temple was torn in two from top to bottom. The earth shook, the rocks split, and the tombs broke open. The bodies of many holy people who had died were raised to life. They came out of the tombs after Jesus' resurrection and went into the holy city and appeared to many people" (Matthew 27:51-53). This passage is packed with fascinating facts.

First, notice that the temple curtain was torn from top to bottom. The curtain was too high to reach with human hands;

this detail shows us that this tearing was clearly an act of God. The temple curtain separated people from the Holy of Holies. God tore down the veil through Jesus' death and gave us full access to Himself. The Bible tells us that we become God's temple because He indwells those who humble themselves with His Holy Spirit.

There is a major difference between Old and New Testament theology and how God cleanses His people. My friend Ron Walborn gave me this great insight through one of his teachings. In the Old Testament, when the "clean" came into contact with the "unclean," the clean became defiled. But in the New Testament, when the clean comes in contact with the unclean, the unclean becomes cleansed. In the New Testament, God's strategy to make us "clean" is to deposit His Holy Spirit right into our hot mess of a life and work on cleaning us up from the inside out. We don't have to get our act together to come to God. We don't have to make ourselves acceptable to God. We don't have to change anything or live a life worthy of God's approval before we can approach Him. We just have to humble ourselves before God and look to Jesus. He tore the veil down so that now unclean people like you and me can come to God, and the Holy Spirit will indwell believers in Jesus and start a holy cleanup. Jesus did that for us because we couldn't do it for ourselves.

> Jesus' death causes dead people to raise to life. Imagine a death so powerful that it broke the chains of death and released life to others!

Second, in what can only be described as one of the most bizarre passages in Scripture, Jesus' death causes dead people to raise to life. Imagine a death so powerful that it broke the chains of death and released life to others! Only Jesus! I suspect this is the moment that Satan and his demonic hosts really knew they were defeated. Up to this point they must have thought they had a chance—they had Jesus tried and crucified. He was dead and buried. The disciples were dismayed and scattered. But when the curtain tore, and the dead saints awakened, Satan must have known He was defeated. Death is Satan's strongest and surest grip. No one can overcome it. Rich and poor, male and female, black and white, every tongue and every tribe, every people group in the world is subject to its long, irresistible reach. The Grim Reaper will come for us all in the end, and it will put us all in a gloomy grave with no options for us to secure our own victory. That's why Jesus came. He came to overcome sin, defeat Satan, and ensure our eternal victory over death. Simply because of His relentless, unstoppable, irresistible tenderness for us.

There is no one like Jesus! He is unparalleled in all of human history. He is the King of the Kingdom. He is the Savior of all who humble themselves and call to Him. He is victor over death. He is the Redeemer of all the weighty ways of the world. He is the tender lover of our souls. You can trust Him.

### Experience

It is time once again to sit alone with Jesus and be still in His presence. Ponder the death of Jesus and what it must have been like for Him. Consider the things I have written here and what it released to you. Humbly come to Jesus and bring Him any shortcomings and sin you need forgiven. Don't wallow in guilt, shame, or condemnation. Just humbly receive all that Jesus has come to give you. Is there any area of your life where you have been going your own way, where it's now time to not only ask Him to forgive, but that you surrender, say yes, and go His way? Allow Him to speak, to reveal anything He wants to you, and humbly trust Him, for He is truly tender, dear ones.

*"The beauty and loveliness of all other things are fading and
perishing; but the loveliness of Christ is fresh for all eternity."*
– JOHN FLAVEL[5]

Five
___

# RESURRECTION APPEARANCES

The entire veracity of the Christian faith rests upon the
resurrection. The Apostle Paul wrote, "If Christ has not
been raised, our preaching is useless and so is your faith" (1
Corinthians 15:14). Paul was convinced of the truth of Jesus'
resurrection because he met the risen Christ on his way to
persecute Christians. That encounter completely changed
Paul's life and purpose. If Jesus isn't alive, then Christianity
is a myth. If the tomb isn't empty, the cross is robbed of its
meaning. There is no victory over sin, death, Satan, and evil;
we are bound, lost, and doomed to live a short life on a broken
planet with no hope of anything beyond this world. That is
pretty dismal. Without the resurrection, Jesus was, at best, a
kindhearted man. Without Jesus' resurrection, Christianity is
no different than any other religion.

The resurrection is what separates Christianity from all other faiths and all other worldviews. The early followers of Jesus were so convinced that Jesus was alive they were willing to die rather than recant what they believed. They all suffered, and most of the apostles were martyred for their faith, but they would not stop talking about Jesus crucified and resurrected. Jesus was their message, their hope, their life, their passion.

I believe in the resurrection because of the apostles' testimony, but also because of my experiences. I follow Jesus because of my encounter with the risen Christ after that breakup: I had a picture in my mind's eye, an inner sense of the Lord speaking to me, and an outpouring of His love that radically altered my life. After my encounter with Jesus, I went into work the next day, and the only other Christian in the workplace saw me walk through the door and said to me, "You've had an encounter with God!" This person could tell. It changed me. I have heard His voice countless times since then. God has conveyed to me things I had no way of knowing—and thousands and thousands of times they have been proven true. Multiple times I have been doing a deliverance and suddenly knew that the person I was doing a deliverance on was conceived in rape. The knowledge helped me complete their deliverance, and in each of those instances I had the person go home and confirm the story with their mother. Every time it was true. I had no way of knowing that; they didn't even know. It was the Spirit of Christ in me talking with me.

I have seen hundreds of people experience miraculous healing. I was praying for an old lady when we were in Brazil together with Randy Clark; I prayed for this woman who had osteoporosis. She couldn't stand up straight. If she bent over, she couldn't get back up without her husband physically straightening her. I prayed for her through Jesus' name, and she was instantly healed and could bend over and straighten up with ease. On that same trip, remember, I prayed for a woman with a tumor and watched it shrink before my eyes as she and her husband burst into tears with shouts of joy!

I was in upstate New York a few years ago, and I was praying for a young woman after a talk on how Jesus came to restore us body, soul, and spirit. This young woman came to church for the first time in her life because she had stage 4 cancer and had no medical hope. I prayed for her and she started feeling heat—she had never been to church before and didn't know that was a regular manifestation of divine healing. I told her that Jesus, who was still alive, had just showed up, and the heat she was feeling was His presence. She burst into tears. Then I sensed the Lord telling me that she had been abused by men. I whispered to her, "I know men have not been kind to you, but Jesus is tender, and He will never treat you that way." Again she burst into tears. Her cancer was healed that day, and that young lady came to know Jesus. I believe Jesus is alive because I have seen Jesus do these sorts of things over and over.

Let's look at the apostles' accounts.

Since so much rides on the resurrection of Jesus, I want to look closely at several resurrection encounters. Once again we will witness the tenderness of Jesus on display with those people who had all their hope in Jesus dashed at the predicted, yet still unexpected, crucifixion. Let's start with Mary Magdalene.

Luke tells us that Jesus had driven seven demons out of Mary (Luke 8:2) and that Mary helped support Jesus and the disciples financially along with some other women (Luke 8:3). "Early on the first day of the week, while it was still dark, Mary Magdalene went to the tomb and saw that the stone had been removed from the entrance" (John 20:1). She went and found Peter and John with this news; they ran to the tomb, and John saw the grave clothes folded there and he believed (John 20:8). Peter and John went back to the others to report that the stone covering the tomb was rolled away and Jesus' body was missing.

Mary, though, stayed at the tomb. "Now Mary stood outside the tomb crying. As she wept, she bent over to look into the tomb and saw two angels in white, seated where Jesus' body had been, one at the head and the other at the foot. They asked her, 'Woman, why are you crying?' 'They have taken my Lord away,' she said, 'and I don't know where they have put him'" (John 20:11-13).

Imagine this from Mary's perspective. Mary had some tormenting evil spirits plaguing her until Jesus came into her life and set her free. It is no wonder, then, that she is a loyal, devout follower of His. Jesus had predicted, multiple times, that He was going to Jerusalem to be crucified and rise again. But as we have considered, this was hard for all his friends and followers to grasp. They had a long-standing doctrinal belief in the prophetic passages of a ruling Messiah. Few rabbis taught this "other view" of a suffering Messiah, even though it appears in the Old Testament. And as I mentioned, they likely figured that Jesus was once again trying to communicate some hidden meaning to them with all this death and resurrection talk, perhaps something like another parable. Then there was this: the ministry of Jesus was so powerful—people like Mary were being set free, delivered, healed, and transformed. Jesus was winsome, loving, powerful, effective, and compelling. Yes, there were people who opposed Him, even hated Him, but God was with Him. Surely Jesus would triumph over His opponents, good would triumph over evil, God would vindicate Him, and the masses would not tolerate His death.

Then, in a whirlwind of confusing events, Jesus is tried, convicted, and crucified, and His followers are left destabilized, confused, and afraid for their lives. They heard his last cry (John 19:30); they saw his side pierced with a spear and watched his bodily fluids pour out (John 19:34). Joseph of Arimathea and Nicodemus took Jesus' body and wrapped it according to Jewish burial customs, and they placed Him in a tomb (John 19:38-42). And with this horrible twist in fate, all their hopes were lost. They had hoped that Jesus was the One, the Messiah, the deliverer of Israel, the Savior of the world. They couldn't see how death could lead to victory. Mary didn't go to the tomb to look for a risen Savior. Mary went to the tomb to grieve for a dead friend.

> Mary didn't go to the tomb to look for a risen Savior. Mary went to the tomb to grieve for a dead friend.

Even after she discovered the stone rolled away, and the tomb abandoned, she just logically assumed someone had taken His body, probably with evil intent. As she wept hysterically, she told the angels she was crying because they had taken away Jesus and she didn't know where He was. At this moment in time, she is so lost, alone, and distraught.

Then Jesus appeared, but she didn't know it was Him. Maybe this was because of the weeping, maybe because of the grief, maybe because God prevented her from understanding at that moment, or maybe because Jesus was in His resurrection body. But Jesus asked her, "'Woman, why are you crying? Who is it you are looking for?'" Mary thought He was the gardener, and she pleaded, 'Sir, if you have carried him away, tell me where you have put him, and I will get him'" (John 20:14, 15). Then Jesus spoke a word that brought clarification to all her confusion and relief to all her grief: "Jesus said to her, 'Mary'" (John 20:16). She cried out "Teacher!" and hugged Him tight. Jesus told her, "Do not hold on to me, for I have not yet ascended to the Father. Go instead to my brothers and tell them, 'I am ascending to my Father and your Father, to my God and your God'" (John 20:17).

Oh, the marvelous tenderness of Jesus on display! He had not even ascended to His Father yet, and He takes the time to comfort Mary because she was so distraught. He tells her to stop holding on to Him so He can go to the Father. He sends her off as the first witness of His resurrection. One of the amazing things about this story is that Jesus first appears to women; in the first century, women were not allowed to legally testify in a court of law! Yet Jesus appears first to them and tells them to go tell the apostles that He is alive. I think that speaks volumes about what Jesus thinks of any sort of gender bias. Jesus doesn't value one gender above another or one race above another. To Jesus, we are all equal. He came to die for us all, and He has tenderness for each one of us—male and female, black and white, Jew and Greek, poor and rich.

**Even in our failures, His tenderness does not fail us.**

Jesus sends Mary off with a message for the disciples. Did you notice that He called them "my brothers"? They have just denied Him, betrayed Him, and abandoned Him, but He speaks of them tenderly, as family. This is the

Jesus I love. Even in our failures, His tenderness does not fail us. Then Jesus tells them, "I am ascending to my Father and your Father, to my God and your God." He includes them in the family. You know that they must feel horrible; they are riddled with shame. Peter had just been boasting about how everyone else might fall away, but not him! He would never blow it, he told Jesus. And then he denies Jesus three times, and Jesus sends him this gentle word of loving acceptance.

Jesus' resurrection proves the authenticity of His message and identity. He is who He said He was, and His message is true. Therefore, He is from the Father, He was with the Father in the beginning, and He is going back to the Father. He is Lord of all, God in the flesh; He and the Father are one. And yet their Lord, the incarnate God, does not condemn them for their worst failure, betraying Him in His darkest hour. He has no condemnation, no animosity, no stern words, only tender love.

We all blow it. We all use words to bring others heartache rather than hope and healing. We all do things that are selfish and painful to those around us. We all violate the law of love, and Jesus' tenderness is available to us just as it was to these early followers. These stories are recorded for us to reveal the nature of Jesus, to show us what He is like. This is how Jesus is—not just with them, but with you and me. We need to bring all our mistakes, all our failures, and all our wrongdoings to Jesus. He can forgive anything we confess; only our unwillingness to humble ourselves prevents us from experiencing Jesus' tenderness. The thing that most often hinders us from receiving Jesus' love is our pride. Too often we are too proud to humble ourselves, to admit we are wrong, to apologize to

God and others. We hold on to our pride and miss out on Jesus' tender, healing, transforming love.

Let's return to the post-resurrection encounters. Later that night, Jesus appeared to the disciples. They were huddled together behind locked doors because they were afraid of the people who killed Jesus! Jesus suddenly appeared in the room and said, "'Peace be with you!' After he said this, he showed them his hands and side. The disciples were overjoyed when they saw the Lord" (John 20:19, 20). Jesus showed them His hands and side because they were afraid He was a ghost. You can't blame them! They had seen Him die; they had no doubt that His death was real. They had seen Him breathe His last and watched the spear pierce His side. Luke's gospel tells us that He asked them for something to eat so He could prove He was human and not a ghost (Luke 24:37-43).

After Jesus convinced them that He was alive and not a ghost, He said to them, "'Peace be with you! As the Father has sent me, I am sending you.' And with that he breathed on them and said, 'Receive the Holy Spirit. If you forgive the sins of anyone, their sins are forgiven; if you do not forgive them, they are not forgiven'" (John 20:21-23). Jesus recommissioned them—right then. They had felt like failures. They felt disqualified because of their betrayal, but Jesus wanted them to know they were forgiven, they were His brothers, God was their Father, and they were qualified for work in the Kingdom of God. They were qualified not because of what they had done but because of their relationship with Jesus, and now He had imparted His Spirit to them.

Ultimately, what qualifies anyone to tell others the good news of the Kingdom of God is that they have humbly received and experienced the tender adoptive love of God, and the Spirit of God dwells within them. The disciples' stark failure in some ways qualified them even more to be messengers of the good news because they now knew, in an entirely new and experiential way, Jesus' tender love and forgiveness. Now they were to tell others what they knew firsthand. I love how honest the disciples are about their failures. That is because they have humbled themselves and experienced forgiveness. Now they are confident they are loved, and that makes them secure enough be open and honest about their lives. Insecure people hide, defend, and refuse to take responsibility, but secure people can be honest, open, and take responsibility for their part of things. That's the power of experiencing Jesus' tender, gracious compassion.

> I love how honest the disciples are about their failures. That is because they have humbled themselves and experienced forgiveness.

Unfortunately, one of the disciples missed out on these resurrection appearances, and that, as you know, was Thomas. Again, let's picture it and experience it all from a human perspective. Let's think about this one. Thomas isn't around, for some reason, but the next time he is together with his friends they tell him, "We have seen the Lord!" Now, imagine this: these are the people you have done life with for the past three years. You have traveled with them, eaten with them, fished with them, hung out with them, argued with them (over who is the greatest), and intensely followed Jesus with them. You have left everything behind to follow Jesus with this like-minded band of believers. You have seen the power of

God together—the blind see, the deaf hear, the lame walk, the demonized are delivered, and even the dead are raised. You experienced the last supper together, the trial, and the crucifixion. And now these people you know so well all tell you that you missed the biggest moment of all—Jesus appeared to them, ate with them, they even touched Him! With enthusiasm they declare that Jesus is alive! You were just with them after the crucifixion. You saw their hopes plummet with yours; you watched them grieve as you grieved. And now you can see this dramatic shift in all of them, all testifying together to the same thing, and all with profound excitement and joy.

I can understand why it would be hard to believe. But this new attitude of unmistakable joy and hope, this new energy and excitement from your friends, ought to at least shake your refusal to believe. But for Thomas, none of it moves him. He stubbornly refuses to believe. The stubborn refusal to humble ourselves hardens our heart and further limits our capacity to experience God. Sadly, we all have done it. Thomas says to his friends, despite all their efforts to convince him, "Unless I see the nail marks in his hands and put my fingers where the nails were, and put my hand into his side, I will not believe" (John 20:25).

God never forces anyone to believe, nor does He force anyone to follow. It takes faith. There is surely ample evidence to believe in Jesus and all He has done for us. I am convinced Jesus is alive today. I believe because of the witness of the apostles—perhaps most of all because they suffered and died for what they believed. But also because they are so humble in their telling of the Gospel accounts; they allow us to see all their flaws. Most people who tell a lie aren't honest and they certainly aren't willing to die for a lie that they propagate. But the apostles were utterly convinced Jesus had risen. If they had made it up, they would have recanted when they were about to die. But clearly, they were so convinced of Jesus' resurrection they would much rather die than recant.

But it isn't just what I have read from the apostles that has convinced me of the resurrection. As I said to start this chapter, I have heard the Lord's voice, and He has revealed things to me I could not have known any other way. I was praying for someone who came to our church for healing, and suddenly I just knew this woman was a witch. I asked her if she had ever engaged in any other religious practices, and she told me she had been a witch for thirteen years. That would count! God healed her, she came to faith in Christ, and her daughter came to faith in Christ and became one of your friends. So many of these stories I tell involve people that you know, and you have seen Jesus' transforming work in their lives. In one of my travels I prayed for a woman whose heart rate was beating so fast you could see her heart pounding through her shirt. The word *abandonment* came to my mind. I asked her if she had been abandoned, and she told me her husband had just left her and that she was abandoned by her father as a child. I prayed that the abandonment wound would be healed and the peace of Christ would come upon her, and immediately her heart came back into a normal rhythm. I could tell hundreds of stories like this one, which I have done in other books, in my preaching, and to our family.

I have prayed in Jesus' name and seen people healed of cancer, back pain, shoulder pain, knee pain, stomach pain, anxiety, depression, and a host of other things. I saw someone cured from brain damage after a deliverance and a time of prayer in Jesus' name. I have witnessed a person get out of a wheelchair in Ecuador after praying in Jesus' name, and they walked across the stage to testify that Jesus heals. I mentioned the tumor, in Brazil, that I saw shrink after prayer in Jesus' name—you four were all there with me for that one, though none of you were standing next to me at the time. I saw a woman's leg grow in a conference that Ron and I did in Connecticut; she had a six-inch platform on one shoe because of a car accident she had been in as a teenager, and that day her leg grew back to its normal length so that she could run again for the first time in nearly two decades. You should have seen her run and shout for joy because of what Jesus did! I could tell you thousands of stories of how Jesus has given me supernatural knowledge or touched someone with His resurrection power. This is why I believe in and love Him so. I have witnessed His risen presence show up and alter someone's unalterable circumstances again and again.

I have also seen Jesus deliver thousands of people from dark spirits and watched the radical difference it has made in their lives. I could tell you stories for days on end about Jesus' power to set people free from all sorts of tormenting demonic strongholds and their symptoms. Earlier this year I was in California and met a woman who had been to a Soul Care Conference a few years earlier. She came up to me with tears in her eyes and said, "I know these stories must get old." But I assure you, as I assured her: they never get old. She went on to tell me that she had suicidal thoughts every day for her entire life. After I did her deliverance in Jesus' name, she has not had a suicidal thought since. She told me she used to drive across bridges and hold onto the steering wheel so tight her knuckles would turn white because she was terrified she would be compelled to drive off the bridge. But today she just enjoys the view as she makes those same drives. Imagine that! Decades of torment—and then dramatic and complete freedom through Jesus. I have prayed for people who have been sexually abused and have perverted dreams at night. Sadly, sometimes they wake up and it feels like someone is having sex with them, but no one is there. It is a demonic encounter, yet I have prayed for thousands of people who have had these symptoms and, after casting out the demons in Jesus' name, all their symptoms are gone—no more perverted dreams, no more nighttime visitors. Can you imagine what this is like for these people? Years of torment taken away through one encounter with Jesus' tender presence. This is why I have no doubt that Jesus rose from the dead, because the Jesus I have read about in the gospels is the Jesus I know in my experience. That's my Jesus, and that's why I love Him and follow Him with my whole heart.

Over the years I have told you many stories like these, and I have spoken about them and recorded many of them in my books. But you have to choose to believe, just like I did. You have to choose to get to know Him and follow Him and develop your own personal history with God. You can't live on my history, but Jesus can create a history with you, and you can know Him as I have known Him. The disciples provided Thomas with overwhelming evidence and testimony that

Jesus was alive, but he refused to believe despite the evidence, despite the change he could plainly see in them.

There is no credit given in the New Testament to the skeptic. The credit in the Bible is always given to those who believe. Sadly, the Evangelical church today too often gives more credit to the skeptic than it does to those who believe. I would urge you: don't be like that. Other people may read my books and write against me and criticize me, and I have even had reviews suggest that I am lying about these stories I tell. But you, my children, know me, and you know I am not making these things up. You know some of the people who have been healed and delivered and transformed. You know Gil Johnson, who was healed of a heart aneurysm after we prayed for him one night; the doctor verified the miracle. You knew John Dreystadt, who was headed into back surgery until some people prayed for him one Sunday morning at church. He never needed the surgery. You know Janis Lemieux, who was miraculously healed one Sunday morning from a stomach ailment. You know Jerry and Anya and Tara, whose lives were transformed through Jesus encounters and deliverance. Too often pastors teach from the Gospels, and they essentially say, "This is who Jesus was and this is what Jesus did." But I testify to you that this is who Jesus *is* and this is what Jesus *does*. I have seen it with my own eyes over and over. He is the same yesterday, today, and forever—because He has risen.

All of Christianity resides in this one truth: if Jesus is alive, He is Lord, and the only proper response is to follow Him. If Jesus is dead, so is our faith. I don't believe that Jesus is alive simply because I read it in the Bible—though that is where my faith begins. I don't only believe that Jesus is alive because the disciples were willing to die for it—though that is a pretty convincing argument that they believed it! I believe Jesus is alive because I have seen what He can do, I have heard His voice, I have experienced His power, and I have tasted His extraordinary tenderness firsthand. I've personally experienced His life-changing power and healing. He has changed me. I am not the person I used to be because of my encounters with the risen Christ.

You must examine what these ancient witnesses have claimed, and what you know about me and what I have claimed, and you must wrestle with who Jesus is and decide if you will follow Him wholeheartedly yourselves. And you must go on to develop your own personal history with God. As for me, I am completely convinced, and Jesus is the most important part of my life. I have centered everything I do on Him. He isn't just at the edges of my life; He is at the center because I know Him. Jesus is simply the most beautiful, most compelling person I know.

I don't follow Jesus when it is convenient or easy or popular. To center my life on Jesus means I follow Him wherever He leads and I seek to do whatever He asks. This is what I hope and pray for you every day. After years of putting Jesus at the center of my life and following hard after Him, I can tell you it is simply the single best decision I have ever made.

Returning to the story of Thomas: a whole week goes by, and this with the disciples undoubtedly talking excitedly about the meaning of Jesus' resurrection and trying to convince Thomas. Still, this one disciple refuses to believe—until Jesus appears again. "A week later his disciples were in the house again, and Thomas was with them. Though the doors were locked, Jesus came and stood among them and said, 'Peace be with you!' Then he said to Thomas, 'Put your finger here; see

157

my hands. Reach out your hand and put it into my side. Stop doubting and believe'" (John 20:26, 27).

Jesus knows us through and through. He knew Thomas was stubbornly refusing to believe, and He knew why. Jesus knew what part of Thomas's unbelief was connected to grief, what part of it was stubbornness, what part of it was hurt, what part was pain, and what part was pride. When He showed up that second Sunday in the upper room, He offered peace first, and then He sought to resolve Thomas's doubt. He offers proof, the very proof Thomas said he needed. Do you see how far Jesus goes to meet Thomas where he is? Jesus knew what Thomas said. Jesus knew what Thomas thought. Jesus knew what Thomas felt. He doesn't come with judgment or condemnation for Thomas. He comes with directness and much-needed correction. Jesus is direct. He is full of grace and full of truth (John 1:14). He doesn't pull any punches or let Thomas off the hook for his stubborn refusal to believe. But He does come ready to resolve his doubt and forgive his refusals. In the end, Thomas doesn't need to put his finger in the nail prints. Rather, he proclaims, "My Lord and my God!" (John 20:28). Jesus says to him, and to us, "Because you have seen me, you have believed: blessed are those who have not seen and yet have believed" (John 20:29).

I went to church from the time I was young. I remember when I prayed to "receive Christ"; I was in second grade. Grandma read a children's Bible with Uncle Ken and me one evening at bedtime, and I prayed for Jesus to be my Savior. Sadly, it didn't make much difference in my life. I think it created some moral restraint in me. Somehow or other, even back then, I knew that one day I would wholeheartedly follow Jesus. And I believed enough that I didn't want to go off the rails! But that was as far as my faith took me until the encounter I had with Jesus after that breakup. That's when I experienced Jesus' tenderness for the first time in a real way. I, like Thomas and the rest of the disciples, realized I had wronged Jesus with my denials, betrayals, and unfaithfulness—and yet He still loved me. He made it plain to me, on that day I surrendered, that I had rejected Him. I realized that my heart was pierced, and I repented. It is really hard to understand and experience the tenderness of Jesus without understanding the extent to which we have blown it in life and failed Him. This is why humility is so important—only with humility can we truly know the depths of God's love. Our society has become more and more a society of blame instead of personal responsibility. People who blame never experience grace; they have an entitlement attitude. They spin rather than take personal responsibility. If you don't take responsibility for your wrongs, you cannot know how much Jesus' death reveals God's love. If it is always someone else's fault, or society's fault, then you have no need of grace and forgiveness, and you have little gratitude. It seems to me that the people who are most judgmental in life are the ones who are least likely to admit their personal shortcomings. They need a grace awakening so they can experience the tenderness of Jesus and extend it to others. But we can't have a grace awakening without understanding our own sinfulness and wrongdoing. Only to the degree we realize our wrongs can we experience God's love.

> This is why humility is so important—only with humility can we truly know the depths of God's love.

You know when I met Jesus that first time, I cried out to Him about my broken heart. "I loved this girl, and look what she did to me!" And I had an image in my mind's eye of Jesus standing there, and I was rejecting Him, and I heard Him say, "That's the same way you have treated me your whole life." Again, He wasn't being mean. He was confronting me with the truth: I had pushed Him to the edges of my life. But that truth pierced my heart, and the piercing of my heart opened me to humble myself and receive His tender love.

You know that the soil here at our house in New York is full of clay. We have the dogwood tree in the yard between the house and the fence, but it is sadly stunted because the clay is so hard the tree can't sink deep roots. It is shorter than it should be and always seems to be limping along. If you want to plant anything here and have it flourish, you have to break through the clay and replace it with soft topsoil. So it is with the human heart. When the heart is hard it must be pierced to be opened to receive the seed from God and then flourish. I had heard about Jesus and the good news my whole life, but on the day that my heart was pierced, the hard places were broken up and the seed took root and began to flourish in my life. Jesus went from the edges to the center, and my life changed forever.

One of the more interesting stories of Jesus' post-resurrection appearances occurs in Luke 24. I find this account so interesting because it is the only one with no "name" players dominating the narrative. All the rest of the appearances are with the apostles or key figures like Mary Magdalene. These are people whose names appear throughout the Gospel accounts as close associates of Jesus. But in Luke 24, not these two, who Jesus meets on the road to a town called Emmaus.

It is the only time we run into them in the Bible. Only one of their names is even revealed to us: Cleopas.

They were walking in Emmaus, about seven miles from Jerusalem, and they were talking about Jesus, His death, the angelic appearance to multiple women, and the empty tomb. At this point they did not know of anyone who had yet seen Jesus. Jesus came up to them on the road and joined their conversation. But Luke tells us "they were kept from recognizing him" (Luke 24:16). Jesus asked, "'What are you discussing together as you walk along?' They stood still, their faces downcast. One of them, named Cleopas, asked him, 'Are you only a visitor to Jerusalem and do not know the things that have happened there in these days?'" (Luke 24:17, 18) It is a funny exchange because they are talking about Him, and He knows that, but He is drawing them into conversation about Himself and they have no idea. So they start explaining things about Jesus to Jesus Himself!

They say to Him, "About Jesus of Nazareth. He was a prophet, powerful in word and deed before God and all the people. The chief priest and our rulers handed him over to be sentenced to death, and they crucified him; but we had hoped that he was the one who was going to redeem Israel. And what is more, it is the third day since all this took place. In addition, some of our women amazed us. They went to the tomb early this morning but didn't find his body. They came and told us that they had seen a vision of angels, who said he was alive. Then some of our companions went to the tomb and found it just as the women had said, but him they did not see" (Luke 24:19-24).

They are so confused. They had hoped Jesus was the One, and now He has died. The women said they had seen a vision of angels who claimed He was alive, and the tomb was empty, but no one had seen Jesus. The whole thing is confusing, upsetting, and grievous to them! And Jesus listens to them pour out their hearts. Tenderly, He listens to their painful emotional processing; Jesus always has space for our emotional upheaval. He doesn't interrupt. He just patiently listens and enters their world. You see, Jesus could have walked up to them and said, "I'm alive!" But He enters their world and helps them process their pain. He gently leads them to understand all that has happened. They can't make sense of it on their own, so He patiently listens, cares, and explains. It has been a twisting tornado of circumstances that has left their faith mangled, and now He has come to help untangle the mess and make sense of the chaos.

After tenderly listening, Jesus starts to bring light to their darkened understanding. "He said to them, 'How foolish you are, and how slow to believe all that the prophets have spoken! Did not the Messiah have to suffer these things and then enter his glory?' And beginning with Moses and all the Prophets, he explained to them what was said in all the Scriptures concerning himself" (Luke 24:25-27). I have studied the Bible my entire life. I have read it cover to cover more than fifty times and read many parts hundreds of times. I have studied in seminary, learned from scholars, read thousands of books on these matters, earned a Masters and Doctorate in theological studies, and I would gladly trade it all for that one conversation with Jesus! I suspect I would have learned more in that one exchange with Him than all the rest of it put together.

Perhaps what is most amazing to me about the tenderness of Jesus in this conversation is the fact that He chose to spend this much time with two "nobodies." We don't even know who they are! But they mattered to Jesus. They never appear again on the pages of Scripture, but Jesus spent this day with them to lift their downcast faces, illuminate their darkened understanding, and clarify their confusion over all that had happened. It is interesting to me that they didn't recognize Him even though they walked with Him, and they couldn't see Him for who He was even though they were students of the Scriptures. It seems to me their physical blindness to His presence in this moment reflects their spiritual blindness in the Scriptures. They were learned men, but ignorant, because they did not have eyes to see or ears to hear what the Scriptures were actually saying to them. They had a preconceived notion of who the Messiah was, and what He would do, and it blinded them to essential truths about Him because who Jesus actually is didn't fit within their theological boxes. Sadly, they are not alone—this same thing is all too common with many of us who grow up in the church and "know" our Bibles.

"As they approached the village to which they were going, Jesus continued on as if he were going farther. But they urged him strongly, 'Stay with us, for it is nearly evening; the day is almost over.' So he went in to stay with them. When he was at the table with them, he took bread, gave thanks, broke it, and began to give it to them. Then their eyes were opened and they recognized him, and he disappeared from their sight. They asked each other, 'Were not our hearts burning within us while he talked with us on the road and opened the Scriptures to us?'" (Luke 24:28-32)

They don't recognize Jesus until He breaks the bread with them, like He did with the twelve apostles at the Last Supper. Suddenly He disappears and they finally have eyes to see and ears to hear! Jesus' tenderness extends to our sinfulness and our ignorance, our stubbornness and our spiritual blindness, our waywardness and our foolishness. Jesus meets us where we are and loves us as we are. If we are careful, we can capture the moments when our hearts are burning within us. These are the moments when God draws near. He is speaking to us, revealing Himself to us, making Himself known to us, but they are moments easy to miss. We can too easily miss out on the opportunity to meet Jesus on the road of life because we are blind to revelation in the Scripture and to recognizing Jesus visiting us in our daily existence, just like these guys on the road to Emmaus.

> Jesus' tenderness extends to our sinfulness and our ignorance, our stubbornness and our spiritual blindness, our waywardness and our foolishness.

Jesus, in His tenderness, is revealing Himself to us, more than we know, and we are missing His appearances more than we realize. Take stock, dear ones, slow down, reflect, and notice where Jesus is appearing in your midst. Notice when your heart burns within you, when the Spirit stirs your soul, and Jesus Himself is drawing near. Notice when a common, ordinary moment becomes a sacred encounter. This is one of the reasons I spend so much time reading Scripture, praying, reflecting, and writing down my thoughts, insights, and reflections in a prayer journal. I do it every day because it is so easy to miss Jesus on the road of life. Like Cleopas and his friend, we think we have already understood the Scriptures, so we miss what He is saying; we think we have correctly interpreted events, and we miss His appearing. Tenderly, patiently, He works with us who are slow to hear and see, trying to help us experience His loving presence along life's way.

\* \* \* \* \*

The final post-resurrection appearance I want to look at with you covers the entirety of John 21. The disciples had gone out fishing. I suspect they were so lost and confused after this whirlwind of events that they simply went back to what was familiar to them. They were still trying to make sense of the crucifixion, the resurrection, all that Jesus had told them, and the Scriptures. Things certainly had not turned out like they had expected—not at all. That is often the way life is, but I can honestly say it is often during the unexpected twists and turns that I have met God in the deepest, most transformational ways. I don't know if I can say that I have come to embrace these topsy-turvy twists in life, but I have at least gotten to the place where I don't despise them because I have frequently experienced God's redeeming hand in them. But I have to tell you, children, God doesn't redeem them without our cooperation. He never forces us to mature, to learn, or to benefit from life's hardships. And I have met far too many people who have not benefited from suffering. Suffering doesn't automatically make us better any more than age automatically makes us mature. I know many people who have suffered without benefit, and many people who have grown old without growing up. The promise, though, that God has made is that He will redeem everything that comes into our life to make us more like Jesus (Romans 8:28-39), and that nothing will be able to separate us from His love. It is a beautiful promise, and I have seen God fulfill it over and over in my life. So we can trust Him no matter what happens in life. Again, I have seen some people benefit from suffering and others become embittered through suffering. Your attitude in hardship makes all the difference. We do not get to choose if we will suffer in life; we only get to choose how we suffer. Learn to suffer wisely, redemptively.

So I suspect that's what the disciples were doing fishing. They were trying to make sense of this radical couple of weeks and the dramatic last few years. They were reflecting, thinking, learning, and processing together. But they also went back to what they did before they met Jesus. Peter and his brother Andrew, James and his brother John—they were all fishermen. But that morning they were in for a surprise.

I'm sure these professional fishermen went to their favorite fishing spots that night, but they caught nothing. Early in the morning someone yelled to them from the shore, "Friends, haven't you any fish?" You're out all night, you catch nothing, and this guy on the shore is calling you out! Dejectedly, they respond, "No." And the man calls, "Throw your net on the right side of the boat and you will find some." They were a little slow to the take, but after throwing their net out and catching a huge load of fish, it finally dawned on John (the writer of the Gospel) that this was Jesus on the shore! After all, they had been through this once before.

When Jesus first called these four fishermen, He had used their boat as a pulpit. They had pushed from shore and Jesus spoke to a crowd. After speaking, Jesus told the four to go into the deep waters and catch some fish. Peter protested, saying that they had been out all night and had caught nothing, but because Jesus told them to do it, they would. And they caught a literal boatload of fish! Peter fell on his knees before Jesus and declared that he was a sinful man, and Jesus called Him to follow Him and to begin to fish for people.

It isn't an accident that Jesus revisits this same scene with them after they had failed this time. He meets them after they had failed at fishing and helps them succeed. He calls them to follow Him, and they fail at their ministry mission through betrayal. Now He takes them back to another failed fishing adventure to remind them of their new mission. He leads them once again to success in fishing, to remind them of their higher calling. That even though they failed as fishermen, and failed as followers, He still loves them, forgives them, and is with them. And in the end, He will help them succeed in following, and in ministry, as He helped them succeed in fishing. Paul writes, "If we are faithless, he remains faithful, for he cannot disown himself" (2 Timothy 2:13). Jesus has more grace than you have sin. He has more tender affections than you have failures.

> Jesus has more grace than you have sin. He has more tender affections than you have failures.

Peter jumps in the water and swims to Jesus while the rest of the disciples follow along in the boat tugging the net full of fish to shore. "When they landed, they saw a fire of burning coals there with fish on it, and some bread" (John 21:9). I love this scene. First, note that Jesus has prepared breakfast for them. They have been out all night, didn't catch anything, which He knew, and He has made them breakfast so they can sit and eat with Him. He cares for us in the smallest details of life.

He also invites them to participate in the feast. "Bring some of the fish you have just caught" (John 21:10). He gives them credit for the catch—even though He was the one who pointed out where the fish were! God always wants to partner with us. Listen: He doesn't need them to bring fish. He already has fish, He knew where the fish were hiding out, and He could have brought plenty more to the party if He wanted. But He invites them to bring what they have. God always invites us to bring what He has given us—our gifts, abilities, talents, and resources—to participate in His Kingdom activity for an eternally significant, fruitful life. He likes partnering with us. I have partnered with God my whole life, and it has been a great joy. Actually, the greatest joy in life is feeling like you have a loving relationship with the God of the universe and are partnering with Him to make a difference that lasts for all eternity. It's remarkable. I am so grateful that God allows me to know Him intimately and participate in His Kingdom-advancing activities. He doesn't have to, but it is a privilege. It creates eternal meaning to life. I have seen God set people free from decades of bondage. I have seen Jesus heal hearts, reconcile relationships, release people from shame, break people's addictions, and deliver people from tormenting spirits. My whole life I have been participating with Jesus in His Kingdom work, and I have seen tens of thousands of lives changed. He didn't have to invite me in, but He did, and my life is saturated with meaning.

Grandma's parents, Nana and Pop Pop Edgett, were lay people in the church. They died when you were pretty young, so you probably don't remember too much about them. They were devout followers. They too participated in God's Kingdom activity. They helped dozens and dozens of people come to know and follow Jesus and find freedom in Christ. Pop Pop was a land surveyor, and later in life they worked together as owners of an antique shop, but their primary love and purpose always revolved around Jesus. As a result, their lives were saturated with eternal significance. They never lost that. I remember going to visit Gram and Pop in the nursing home when they were in their eighties and they were talking about leading a Bible Study with some of the residents who were not Christ followers. They wanted to serve Jesus and help others come to know Him even at their advanced age. So Jesus invites the apostles—and us—to share in His eternal service. This real relationship and Kingdom service brings ultimate meaning to our lives. He didn't have to, but He chose to, and this is part of the tenderness of Jesus: wanting our lives to be filled with everlasting significance. When your life is filled with meaning, the significance you derive from it gives you passion and a reason to get out of bed in the morning with excitement and joy.

The other thing noteworthy in the story is that Jesus was cooking the fish on a coal fire. That isn't an accident. There are only two times the word for coal fire appears in the New Testament. Here and in John 18:18, where Peter was warming himself around a fire of coals the night he denied that he knew Jesus. It would have been a lot easier to find wood along a beach than it would have been to find coal, but Jesus intentionally lights a coal fire as part of His coordinated move to help heal Peter's soul.

Jesus has to restore Peter because Peter is utterly demoralized. When you read the Gospels, it is pretty obvious that Peter is the spokesman of the group, the leader, and he has fallen badly. He is heartbroken, ashamed, confused, defeated, and beat down. He feels unworthy, incompetent, embarrassed, and disqualified. Part of why he likely went back to fishing is because he feels so inadequate to follow Jesus and fulfill his God-given mission with people. He simply feels like he has tried and failed; he just can't do it. So Jesus takes Peter back to the scene of his calling—fishing all night and catching nothing until Jesus shows him where to find fish. He takes him back to the scene of his failure: a coal fire. You know that as Peter sat there by the fire that morning watching the coal burning, he was thinking about the night of his betrayal. Plus, this is the third time (John 21:14) that Jesus appeared to the disciples, and Peter denied Jesus three times. None of it is an accident. This is the well-orchestrated touch of our tender Savior to bring Peter back from the scrap pile of human failure. Few things create shame like failure, and we cannot overcome shame without bringing our failure into the light with God and others. We need to bring our failure under the umbrella of love without judgment. That's what Jesus is doing for Peter.

They eat their breakfast, and then Jesus begins a painful but necessary conversation. "Jesus said to Simon Peter, 'Simon son of John, do you love me more than these?'" (John 21:15). People have debated through the centuries whether Jesus meant *more than these fish or more than these disciples,* but I suspect Jesus meant *more than these other disciples love me.* After all, Peter had declared that even if everyone else fell away, he would remain faithful. But he had failed. Peter responds, "Yes, Lord, you know that I love you" (John 21:15). You may have heard people make a big deal of the Greek words used here for love. Jesus asks Peter if he "*agapes* me," and Peter responds that he "*phileos*" Jesus. But honestly, as I study John's use of these two words, he uses them interchangeably at times; he even uses *phileo* to describe the Father's love for the Son. So I'm not sure we can make a big deal of the Greek words for love that Jesus uses. But I *am* sure that this is the most important question Jesus could ask any of us: Do you love me?

Jesus had told them that the most important thing was love. Love God, love people. Loving Jesus is the only proper response for one who has understood the tender love He has for us. Jesus died for Peter; He has proven His love for Peter. Now He only wants to know one thing: "Do you love me?" After Peter responds that he does, Jesus tells him, "Feed my lambs" (John 21:15). Jesus is saying: it is time to get back to the calling, Peter. Yes, you have failed, but my grace runs deeper than your failure. My love is greater than your sin.

> Loving Jesus is the only proper response for one who has understood the tender love He has for us.

Again, picture this scene in your head. All the disciples are there. They are watching. Peter is undoubtedly feeling the heat after his colossal failure. They have been arguing the whole time over who is the greatest, and Peter was in the running, but after this . . . could he even get back up? Jesus pressed in and asked a second time, "'Simon son of John, do you love me?' He answered, 'Yes, Lord, you know that I love you.' Jesus said, 'Take care of my sheep'" (John 21:16). All the others are awkwardly watching this exchange. They all have failed. They all feel bad. Peter isn't alone in his need for restoration, but he is the spokesman, he is the leader, and he will not get back in the saddle unless he overcomes his shame. Peter feels bad because Jesus is putting him on the spot before his friends, and they feel bad because they are probably wondering if they will be next!

Peter, I am sure, cannot wait for this interaction to end, but Jesus isn't done yet. Three times Peter denied Him. Three times Jesus asked the question. "'Simon son of John, do you love me?' Peter was hurt because Jesus asked him the third time, 'Do you love me?' He said, 'Lord, you know all things; you know that I love you.' Jesus said, 'Feed my sheep'" (John 21:17).

The greatest problem in the church today is that we are making it too much about us. We make it too much about our wants, our needs, our desires, our opinions, and not enough about Jesus. This is indicative of the fact that Jesus is at the edges of our life, not at the center. But if Jesus is who He claimed, and we are merely here on earth for less than a century, then we really ought to make life far more about Jesus and His eternal Kingdom. He ought to be the center of it all, not merely a part of it all. The most important question in all the world comes down to this: do you love Jesus? If so, do His bidding. Peter's bidding was to shepherd God's flock. Love Jesus and do what He wants. That's pretty much the secret to life. I have always said to you: the secret to life is to find what God wants and do it. If you love Jesus and do what He wants, your life will be more fulfilled. You will be more free and full. You will experience more of God's favor and presence. You will find more joy and peace. Find what God wants and do it. Love Jesus and do His bidding. You know one of the things I love about God is that, in His tenderness for us, He simplifies life to these basic things: love God, love people, find what God wants, and do it. We tend to make life so complicated, and we get overwhelmed and distressed. Jesus tenderly comes to us in our disturbed state and brings us back to the basics. His burden is easy; His yoke is light.

Jesus then speaks to Peter about the death that awaits him. "'Very truly I tell you, when you were younger you dressed yourself and went where you wanted, but when you are old you will stretch out your hands, and someone else will dress you and lead you where you do not want to go.' Jesus said this to indicate the kind of death by which Peter would glorify God. Then he said to him, 'Follow me!'" (John 21:18, 19) Peter eventually died on a cross, just like Jesus, and this time he rose to the occasion; he didn't deny Jesus, and he died the noble death of a martyr.

But in this moment, Peter couldn't help wondering about the others, especially John. Still making it too much about himself, Peter compares himself with John. He asked, "'Lord, what about him?' Jesus answered, 'If I want him to remain alive until I return, what is that to you? You must follow me'" (John 21:21, 22). Love God, love people. Find what God wants and do it. Don't worry about other people and their lives. Don't envy. Don't compare yourself with others and their lot in life. All these things just complicate life and rob us of our peace. In the end, Peter gets it. He makes it less about him and more about Jesus. He loves Jesus to the end, and he dies for Jesus with courage. Jesus tenderly restored Peter back to the place where he needed to be, focused on the One he needed to be focused on, doing the things he needed to be doing, and saying yes to Jesus no matter what.

Jesus appeared to His disciples over a period of forty days (Acts 1:3), and He spoke to them about the Kingdom of God. Then one day He told them to "wait for the gift my Father promised, which you have heard me speak about. For John baptized with water, but in a few days you will be baptized with the Holy Spirit" (Acts 1:4, 5). In His final conversation with the disciples, He promises them the coming of the Holy Spirit, the Comforter. Though Jesus would no longer be physically present with them, He would be present with them permanently through His Spirit. They would not be alone; they would not be orphaned. No matter what they went through from then on, He would be with them. No matter what hardship they faced, they would not face it alone. No matter what temptations and struggles confronted them, He would be with them to help them overcome. He would be with them to empower them for their Kingdom mission. The Holy Spirit would indwell them, lead them, guide them, help them witness, empower them, and speak to them (Acts 1:5, 2:17f). "After he said this, he was taken up before their very eyes, and a cloud hid him from their sight. They were looking intently up into the sky as he was going, when suddenly two men dressed in white stood beside them. 'Men of Galilee,' they said, 'why do you stand here looking into the sky? This same Jesus, who has been taken from you into heaven, will come back in the same way you have seen him go into heaven'" (Acts 1:9-11).

Tenderly, Jesus lived with them; tenderly, Jesus died for them; tenderly, Jesus appeared to them; tenderly, Jesus departed them. This is who Jesus *is* and this is what Jesus *does*. He hasn't changed. The Spirit of Jesus is still with us and accessible to us. He can still comfort, console, and tenderly minister Jesus' loving presence to us day by day. This has been my experience for nearly four decades as I have walked with Jesus. There is no one like Jesus. He is simply the most beautiful, most tender, most admirable person I know. This is my Jesus, and I long for you to know Him as I have known Him, my dearly loved children.

## Experience

Sit quietly alone with Jesus again. He is still alive. He is with you and here to help you, speak to you, and empower you. Talk to Him about where you are on your spiritual journey. Thomas stubbornly refused to believe. Peter was crippled with failure. Mary was grief-stricken and heartbroken. Where are you? Talk to Him about your heart's condition, and then quietly linger with Him. Humble yourself, listen, and receive.

# CORRECTIVE LENSES

*"No pen, no words, no image can express to you*
*the loveliness of my only, only Lord Jesus."*
–THE LOVELINESS OF CHRIST, SAMUEL RUTHERFORD[6]

*"O if only you knew his worth and excellency,*
*what he is in himself, what he has done for you,*
*and deserved from you, you would need no arguments*
*of mine to persuade you to love him!"*
– JOHN FLAVEL[7]

I began the book by talking about the two lenses that have been distorting our view: the lens of the problem of evil and the lens of religion (and the sins committed by church people). These lenses have caused us to struggle with the goodness of God and resulted in a great deal of deconstruction that is taking place in the church. As I said earlier, we need to deconstruct the church in its various forms so we can reconstruct something that will help generate a fresh move of God. But sadly, too often we have ended up deconstructing Jesus and are left standing in a pile of rubble.

If deconstruction is going to end up being constructive—or, reconstruction—then we need new lenses to view the world. We need to replace the lens of the fall (the problem of evil) and the lens of religion with the lens of the cross and the lens of eternity.

## The Lens of the Cross

We will never understand or experience the goodness of God and the tenderness of Jesus without viewing this fallen world through the lens of the cross. As you have often heard me say before, and in this book, on the cross Jesus entered our pain and suffering, He suffered with us, and He suffered for us. The cross is the ultimate proof that God is good, and God is for us. God didn't stand aloof and indifferent to all our pain and suffering. He didn't sit safely removed from pain in Heaven and cavalierly ignore our heartache. He became one of us, and joined us in our fallen, broken, dysfunctional world full of evil, suffering, sin, and pain. The only motivating reason for Jesus enduring the cross is His tender love. Paul said, "What, then, shall we say in response to these things? If God is for us, who can be against us? He who did not spare his own Son, but gave him up for us all—how will he not also, along with him, graciously give us all things?" (Romans 8:31, 32)

> Through the cross meaning emerges from our suffering. God can redeem our suffering to make us more like Jesus.

The cross makes sense of suffering. Through the cross meaning emerges from our suffering. God can redeem our suffering to make us more like Jesus (Romans

8:28-39). We can draw near to Jesus through suffering; we can experience His presence and love in suffering. We can enter into the fellowship of His suffering (Philippians 3:10).

When I look through the lens of the cross, I understand that sin has distorted the world, and the world is not working the way God intended it to work. I understand that pain, suffering, injustice, sin, brokenness, and dysfunction are not part of God's original plan. They are the results of people's sinful choices and the consequences of a broken planet. But I also understand that I am not left hopeless in the midst of suffering. God can redeem it; He can make good from it. God can draw near to me in it; He can make me more mature through it. God is so good that even when evil touches my life, when God touches the evil, God can do something good in me. And He can use the comfort I received from Him in that pain to comfort others (2 Corinthians 1). This gives me hope in all things. It makes meaning out of all things. It brings redemptive meaning and purpose to the pain of life.

I told you that in the middle of the marriage crisis God called me to give Him thanks for it. He told me that one day I would be grateful for it. I couldn't see it at the time, but I chose to look through the lens of the cross, I chose to believe that God could redeem it, I claimed Romans 8:28-39, and I gave thanks in faith. Now I can look back and see how hundreds of thousands of people around the world have benefited from that marriage crisis and the things God showed me because of it. It's easy to see how God can redeem something when you get to the other side of suffering, but in the middle of the pain you must look through the lens of the cross.

When I was at the beginning of the attacks at church, I went to the monastery one day and asked the Lord, "Why?" I wasn't complaining. I was just asking why people were acting like this; it was bewildering to me. I heard the Lord say, "I'm answering your prayers." I said, "Lord, I don't know what I have been praying, but if you tell me, I promise I'll stop!" He reminded me that for most of my adult life I had been praying, "Lord, give me the ability to impart your Spirit, like the apostles, if my character and intimacy can sustain it." I had studied Scripture and studied revivals, and I noticed that both in the Bible and in outpourings of God's Spirit, He would give people the ability to lay hands on others and see miracles, see people filled with the Spirit, and encounter God in life-altering ways. I prayed that God would let me do that—but only if my character and intimacy could sustain it. I didn't want to experience more power than I could handle and blow up my life and disgrace Jesus. That day the Lord said to me, "This is what it takes for that prayer to be answered." I had to enter the fellowship of Jesus' sufferings before I could experience Jesus' resurrection power. Jesus had to experience the cross before the resurrection, and so often this is our path to more of God too; we must experience the cross before we experience Jesus' resurrection power. After years of suffering attacks, and then a long, dark night of the soul where I had no sense of God's presence, I came out of that season and God came with power. I saw far more healings, and I have seen thousands of people I prayed for filled with the Holy Spirit in demonstrative, life-changing ways. In the middle of the attacks I couldn't see it; I had to look through the lens of the cross and trust the God of the cross. Now, after God redeemed that suffering, it is easy to see and be grateful for what He has done.

One of the things so important to your trust in God is that you develop a personal history with God. The more you see

God redeem your current suffering, the more you will trust Him in your future crisis. The more you look through the lens of the cross and see how God has created something beautiful out of something painful, the more you will have faith to face your next dark hour.

## The Lens of Eternity

If we are going to experience the tenderness of Jesus and trust God amid the evil that has impacted our world, we must also look through the lens of eternity. We will never make sense of life without factoring in eternity. There are times in life when evil triumphs over good. There are moments where the darkness seems to overwhelm the light. We pray for people we love, yet sickness triumphs and they die. We pray for justice in an unjust circumstance, yet justice never comes. We fight hard to overcome some horrible evil, yet the evil continues. We pray for someone we love to break free from an addiction or toxic pattern of behavior, but they don't break free. I would love to see sex trafficking, racism, gender bias, domestic violence, and sexual abuse eliminated in my lifetime, along with a host of other evils. But sadly, it will not happen, nor will it happen in your lifetime. Wars will continue because evil political rulers will gain power, and self-interest will rule over the common good. Corruption will continue to be the norm because people are sinful, selfish, and greedy. Today we have so much knowledge about all these evil things happening in the world around us. What do we do with it all?

There is a day coming, the Bible tells us, when God will have the last word. The final act in history will be good triumphing over evil for the final time. Evil will be eliminated in the end. John wrote the book of Revelation in a time of persecution. Believers were suffering under the weight of an evil Caesar; many were being persecuted and even martyred for their faith. John had a vision (while he was in prison because of his faith in Jesus) about the ultimate victory of Jesus and the triumph of good over all the evil in the world. John wrote, "Then I saw 'a new heaven and a new earth' for the first heaven and the first earth had passed away, and there was no longer any sea. I saw the Holy City, the new Jerusalem, coming down out of heaven from God, prepared as a bride beautifully dressed for her husband. And I heard a loud voice from the throne saying, 'Look! God's dwelling place is now among the people, and he will dwell with them. They will be his people, and God himself will be with them and be their God. He will wipe every tear from their eyes. There will be no more death or mourning or crying or pain, for the old order of things has passed away'" (Revelation 21:1-4). That's when evil will be eliminated once and for all.

The tenderness of Jesus will ultimately result in His triumph over evil. As we discussed earlier, Jesus is tender for both the oppressed and the repentant oppressors of life. So often the current oppressors were once the oppressed themselves; hurting people hurt others. "A bruised reed He will not break, and a smoldering wick he will not snuff out, till he leads justice to victory" (Matthew 12:20). Jesus is leading us to victory over evil, but He is patiently producing His final triumph. He is patient so that every wayward son and daughter can find their way home. He is so patient because His tenderness is so relentless. He has tenderness for you and me—when we are victims of other people's evil deeds, and when we are the cause of other people's suffering because of our selfish acts. He has been patient with me when I have pushed Him to the edge of my life, and He is patient with you when you have pushed Him to the edge of your life. This is what Jesus is like, and this is why I love Him.

## Personal Encounters with Jesus

I was recently at a Soul Care Conference in Connecticut and on Saturday, as usual, I was leading people through deliverance. I always ask people a series of questions about their life so I can tell what I am looking for and what sort of spirits may be present that they need to be set free from. I must have done more than thirty deliverances that afternoon, and over and over I listened to stories of lives that had been marred by sexual abuse, violence, addiction, witchcraft, emotional abuse, bullying, rape, and other horrible things. I listened, cast out demonic spirits that plagued people through their lifetimes, and prayed tenderly over people who carried an overload of pain and shame. I started praying with all the pastors in the room who needed deliverance—there were more than a dozen of them—and then went on to help many others. One of the pastors, who I did deliverance on, sat by my side all afternoon and into the evening as I continued to minister to dozens of people. At one point he looked at me and said, "How do you do this? You do this all over the world; you listen to all these stories of horrible pain. How do you keep ministering to all this pain without burning out, and with such compassion?" I said to him, "I am not naturally a compassionate person. The compassion I feel comes from Jesus. And He has an endless well of compassion to give. So as long as I stay connected to Him, the compassion doesn't run out. If I have to generate it myself, I will hit my own limits and run out. But Jesus has unending tenderness; I just need to tap into His stream." The unending tenderness of Jesus: that's what we need.

People often come up to me at a conference and say, "I feel like I know you because I've read your books." I write honestly, openly, and vulnerably, so people feel like they know me. But they don't really know me—not like Mom or you or my friends know me. As I said earlier, there is a difference between transparency and vulnerability. In my books I am transparent, but I am not opening myself up to these people in the same way I open myself up with a friend when I talk to that person about my sin or pain. When I open myself up like that, I am expecting something in return; I am expecting love, acceptance, tenderness, support, and understanding. But with these readers, while I am being transparent, I expect nothing in return. Only when we expect something from someone we open ourselves up to do we experience true vulnerability; we take a risk and open ourselves to hurt because we are expecting something in return. If they don't respond as we expect, we are hurt. That's true vulnerability. If I am transparent with you, but hide behind a wall of self-protections, I can remain invulnerable.

It isn't enough to know about the tenderness of Jesus; we must experience the tenderness of Jesus. And that requires vulnerability. We must open ourselves up to Him, trust Him, and risk our heart with Him. We must trust Him with our heartaches and our

> It isn't enough to know about the tenderness of Jesus; we must experience the tenderness of Jesus. And that requires vulnerability.

pain, our sin, and our failings. This is the only way we can experience His tenderness. I have experienced Jesus' tenderness most often in my life through my failures, sin, pain, and suffering. I have experienced Jesus' tenderness most often in life when I have been deeply in need and opened myself up to Him vulnerably.

The problem with vulnerability in a broken world is that we get hurt. We get hurt by people and we feel hurt by God too. I have had to process my hurt often to keep my heart soft and open to others and God. I made a decision some years ago that I would not take offense at God anymore. He had proven His love for me on the cross; He had redeemed hardship over and over in my life. I wasn't going to require God to prove Himself trustworthy any longer, so I made a covenant with God that I would never take offense against Him again. That means I live with a continuous vulnerability with Jesus, but it opens my heart to receive more of His tender affections. I have found He is faithful, and His tenderness knows no bounds. It means I have to process all my disappointments and heartaches so I don't close my heart to God to protect myself and become invulnerable again. The only way I know how to receive His tenderness is to keep my heart open and vulnerable before Him.

This has been my experience with the relentless tenderness of Jesus. Looking back on my life, I realize I have often encountered the tenderness of Jesus in other people. For example, I experienced the Lord's compassion through my first-grade teacher, Miss Shaw. I had separation anxiety, and it was always difficult for me to go to school as a result. Going to school made me feel anxious, and first grade was my first experience with a full day of school, but Miss Shaw's loving, gentle, welcoming presence made my transition to full-time school much easier. Years later I discovered she was a follower of Jesus, and I realized I had experienced the tenderness of Jesus through her. Courtney, you experienced that same tenderness of Jesus through Mrs. Brennan-Ring; she too was a follower of Jesus, and she showed you the tenderness of Jesus when you went to first grade, just as Miss Shaw did with me.

I have experienced the tenderness of Jesus through others often in a time of heartache. Of course, most often, it was people who caused the heartache, and it was not uncommon for Jesus to reveal His tenderness to me through other people to help heal the pain. After that breakup, where I experienced Jesus' love through direct revelation, I also experienced great comfort through a small group that I joined. It was a Bible Study led by a man named Frank, and there were people from many different churches attending. They often cared for me, loved me, and ministered to me in my loneliness. They adopted me into their friend group. They invited me to go with them on vacation. There were two young married couples who especially took me in. One woman, named Chris, particularly made me feel loved, accepted, and special; the tenderness of Jesus demonstrated through her helped heal my broken heart. She died this past year after a bout with cancer, and I regret that I didn't get to see her before she died. But when I get to Heaven and see her again, I will be sure to give her thanks! She represented the love of Jesus so well to me and to many others.

When Mom and I struggled through a marriage crisis in the early years, I received a timely prophetic phone call at midnight one evening from one of the new believers in our church, Jan Jones. The call came on one of my worst nights. I was feeling so hurt and so hopeless, and Jesus told Jan to call me at midnight with a timely word. It was Jesus' way of letting me know that He saw the heartache and pain, and He cared. This is one of the reasons it is important to be in a community of believers, because Jesus often demonstrates his love to us through them.

The first twelve years that I pastored South Shore Community Church went pretty smoothly. The church was growing, the ministry was fulfilling, the people were united. The attacks came after I sensed God calling me to preach on revival. Someone created an imaginary person on Facebook, friended everyone in the church, and started writing against me. I didn't know who it was and couldn't do anything about it. It was so painful, but the tenderness of Jesus was on display once again.

One morning I was spending time alone with the Lord, and I sensed the Lord telling me that this person was going to contact the District Superintendent (the Bishop). I called the district office to talk to the DS, told him what was happening, and said that the Lord revealed to me that this guy was going to contact him. The DS was quiet on the other end of the call. I said, "He already contacted you, right?" The man had written an email that morning! The Lord had prompted me on the day the man wrote to the DS to call the superintendent. I tried to get the DS to help me; I just wanted to confront this individual who was attacking me and dividing the church. He wouldn't, but in the end, the individual wasn't able to meet with the superintendent. But most important of all, I knew Jesus saw and Jesus cared. He had my back, and He was demonstrating His loving care for me in this dark season of life. My life has been filled with these kinds of experiences with Jesus' tender love.

It was during that time that I also started meeting with people on Friday evenings to do a prayer watch; we would pray into the late hours of the night. While it was a heartbreaking season to be attacked and see the church divided because of the attacks, I cannot tell you how Jesus drew near to me during those days. I cannot tell you how often I experienced His tender, healing love. Frequently on those Friday nights I would sense His presence, hear His voice, and experience His love. It was beautiful. Often one of the people present would have a prophetic word for me that released Jesus' tender love to me. Sometimes someone like Janis Lemieux would sing prophetic songs over me, and my heart was soothed under the loving care of Jesus.

One day Miss Mary came up to me at church, and she was sobbing. I had no idea why she was weeping; I just opened my arms and hugged her. I figured something terrible happened to upset her. Then through her sobs she said, "I . . . am . . . weeping . . . for you . . . for the way we have treated you." I lost it. We stood there that Sunday morning weeping together in an embrace. It was so healing for my soul as I experienced the tenderness of Jesus through her tears.

I have felt Jesus' healing love through life's darkest seasons. I have experienced His tenderness correcting me when I've been on a wrong path, healing me when I have been wounded by others, comforting me when life didn't work out the way I hoped, and strengthening me when I wanted to quit in the weariest times. I encountered Jesus' love for the first time when I was 19 after that breakup. As I said earlier, the breakup was mostly my fault; it was my selfishness that caused much pain in our relationship. But even though I was in pain because of my bad choices, Jesus was tender with me. That's the way He is.

I experienced Jesus' tenderness throughout the difficult marriage crisis and throughout the ministry attacks. Often at the monastery, alone with God, I would pour out my heart to Jesus and He would reveal Himself to me once again, full of love and full of truth. I have met the Lord's tender touch in Scriptures that He has illuminated to me, in dreams, pictures, and encounters with Him. I experienced the tenderness of Jesus through others and for others who were carrying heartache and pain. I have done my part in my relationship with Jesus, though far from perfectly. But I kept pursuing and spending time with Him. I kept processing sorrow and suffering; I kept being open and honest with God and others. I have done my part by continually trying to empty the suitcase of the soul with the help of God so my heart would not grow hard toward Him or take offense. What I want you to know is that He will meet you as He has met me if you come after Him as I have done. This is who Jesus is. This is what Jesus does.

You need to know and experience Jesus' tenderness for yourself. And that is my prayer for you. I pray this book will help you see Jesus for who He is. I pray that you will not just know that Jesus is tender and loving, but that you will experience the fullness of Jesus' tender affections. Seek Him, children. There is no one like Jesus. He is truly the most compelling, most beautiful, most tender person in the world.

I had a dream recently that Courtney had died. But her spirit was still alive, and she was talking to me. Her body was a corpse, but in the dream it was like we were trying to find her a new body. It was a weird dream and a sad dream; I woke up crying. I woke up before the dream was finished, and when

I woke up, I just wanted to tell Courtney: "Call out to Jesus! Call out to Jesus!" It's never too late. Call out to Jesus: He can raise your body and give you life again, or He can overcome death and welcome you to Heaven. But with Jesus it is never too late. The tenderness of Jesus is always sufficient, whether for this life or the next, in the face of life's hardships or death's certainty. The tenderness of Jesus is enough for all of it. The tenderness of Jesus is your light in the darkest hour, it is your healing in the most searing pain, it is your cleansing in your worst choices, it is your strength in your greatest weakness. There is no one like Jesus. This is the Jesus that I know, my dear ones, and this is the Jesus that I love! You can trust Him. Follow Him with all your heart. There is no one like Him. Call out to Jesus, children. This is the cry of my heart for you in life and death. Cry out to Jesus, the Tender One of God.

*With all the tender affections of Jesus,*
*Your loving Father*

# Endnotes

1. *The Loveliness of Christ* (GLH Publishing, Louisville, Kentucky), p. 18. Originally published 1909. This work is in the public domain.

2. *Christ Altogether Lovely,* John Flavel, page 2. This work is in the public domain.

3. Flavel, p. 15.

4. *The Loveliness of Christ*, p. 6.

5. Flavel, p. 5.

6. *The Loveliness of Christ*, p. 37.

7. Flavel, p. 18.

# ABOUT THE AUTHOR

Rev. Dr. Rob Reimer is the founder of Renewal International, which he began to fulfill his call to advance the Kingdom of God through personal and corporate spiritual renewal. His books *Soul Care, Spiritual Authority, Deep Faith, River Dwellers, Pathways to the King* and *Calm in the Storm* have sold worldwide. Rob mentors Christian leaders, and his conferences have helped thousands of Christians find freedom and fullness in Christ. Personally transparent, Rob relates lessons learned as he has walked with God, responded to His Word, and processed pain in marriage and ministry. These lessons are not only taught, but participants actively begin the process of incorporating them into their lives, walking in the light, practicing hearing from God, and accessing His power for ministry.

Currently, Dr. Reimer is the Professor of Pastoral Theology at Alliance Theological Seminary in New York, where he earned his Master of Divinity degree. He also holds a Doctor of Ministry in Preaching from Gordon-Conwell Theological Seminary.

To access eCourse, live, or video teaching on *Soul Care*, or to explore more of Rob's work, view his itinerary, or to invite him to speak, please visit www.DrRobReimer.com.

# ALSO BY DR. ROB REIMER

## River Dwellers
### *Living in the Fullness of the Spirit*

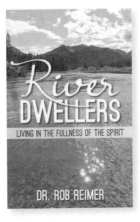

Did you ever wish there was more to your Christian life? Too often the Christian life is reduced to going to church, attending meetings, serving God, and doing devotions. But Jesus promised us abundant life—a deep, intimate, satisfying connection with the living God. How do we access the abundant life that Jesus promised? The key is the presence and life of the Holy Spirit within us.

Jesus said that the Spirit of God flows within us like a river —He is the River of Life. But we need to dwell in the River in order to access the Spirit's fullness.

In *River Dwellers,* Dr. Rob Reimer offers a deep look at life in the Spirit and provides practical strategies for dwelling in the River of Life. We will explore the fullness of the Spirit, tuning into the promptings of the Spirit, walking in step with the Spirit, and developing sensitivity to the presence of God in our lives. This resource will guide you toward becoming a full-time river dweller, even in the midst of life's most difficult seasons when the river seems to run low.

Together let's become River Dwellers, living where the fullness of God flows so that we can carry living water to a world dying of thirst!

## Pathways to the King

### *Living a Life of Spiritual Renewal and Power*

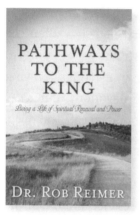

We need revival. The church in America desperately needs revival. There are pockets of it happening right now, but we need another Great Awakening. About forty years ago, the church was impacted by the church growth movement. The goal of the movement was to get the church focused on the Great Commission—taking the Good News about Jesus to the entire world. The church was off mission, and the movement was a necessary course correction. But it didn't work. Many people came to Christ as a result of this outreach emphasis, and I am grateful for that. More churches are now focused on evangelism, helping people come to know Jesus, than they were before the movement. But we have fewer people attending church now (percentage-wise) than ever before in the history of the United States. We need revival.

This book is about how we can usher in revival and also about the price that we must pay to experience it. I believe we have a part to play in seeing the next great spiritual awakening. God wants us to be carriers of His kingdom. He wants us to experience the reality and fullness of His kingdom, and he wants us to expand the kingdom to others—just like Jesus did. In order to do that, I believe we must follow 8 Kingdom Pathways of Spiritual Renewal: Personalizing our Identity in Christ, Pursuing God, Purifying Ourselves, Praising, Praying Kingdom Prayers, Claiming Promises, Passing the Tests, and Persisting. These eight pathways are discussed in great detail, are securely rooted in biblical truths, and are illustrated by compelling examples from Scripture and from my life, the lives of believers in my community, and in the lives of great Christians throughout history.

Available at www.DrRobReimer.com

# Deep Faith

## *Developing Faith That Releases the Power of God*

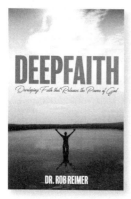

Jesus said, "Very truly I tell you, all who have faith in me will do the works that I have been doing, and they will do even greater things than these" (John 14:12). The extraordinary promise of Jesus is that we can do Kingdom works that He did—cast out demons, heal the sick, save the lost and set the captives free.

Jesus wants to advance His Kingdom through us. But this promise comes with a condition: the level of our Kingdom activity is dependent upon our faith.

There are promises in Heaven that God wants to release, but they cannot be released without faith. There are miracles that God wants to do that cannot be done without faith. There are answers to prayer that God wants to unleash that cannot be unleashed without faith. There are works of the Kingdom that God wants to accomplish that cannot be accomplished unless the people of God develop deeper faith. But there is hope for all of us, because faith can be developed.

Faith opens doors and creates opportunities for accessing God's power against all odds. Faith is a difference maker, a future shaper, a bondage breaker, a Kingdom mover. In this book, Dr. Rob Reimer challenges readers to develop deep faith that can release the works of the Kingdom. Faith is not static; it is dynamic. We can and must take an intentional path toward developing our faith if we want to see the works of the Kingdom in greater measure.

# Spiritual Authority

## *Partnering with God to Release the Kingdom*

Jesus gave His disciples authority to preach the good news of the kingdom of God and to cast out demons, heal the sick, save the lost, and set the captives free. Everywhere Jesus went, the kingdom came with power. There was no proclamation of the gospel without a demonstration of power. It was the authentic demonstration of Jesus' power through His followers that ignited the greatest spiritual movements in the first century. Today, we are becoming more like the spiritual climate in the first century then like 1950 America. In a pluralistic, syncretistic society where all deities are considered equal, only the unequal display of Jesus' power will convince people of the supremacy of Christ. The key to demonstrating the power of the King is authority, and authority is not just positional; it is developmental. Spiritual authority is rooted in identity, expanded in intimacy, and activated by faith. This book takes an in-depth look at how we can grow in identity, intimacy and faith so that we can develop our authority and release the Kingdom.

Also available in Spanish (Autoridad Espirituald).

Available at www.DrRobReimer.com

# Calm in the Storm

## *How God Can Redeem a Crisis to Advance His Kingdom*

There is nothing like a crisis to reveal the cracks in the walls of our soul. But God promises to redeem all things that come into our lives to make us more like Jesus. We are experiencing a unique crisis in our day and age, COVID-19. It has created fear, death, and will leave economic disaster in its wake. In this book, I don't just want to talk about how we can survive this crisis, or how we can access the peace of God in tumultuous times. I want to talk about how God can redeem a crisis in our personal lives to take us deeper into maturity and intimacy with Christ. And how this particular crisis could potentially lead to revival if the church processes it well. We stand on the precipice of an unprecedented opportunity to be purified and mobilized on mission to advance the Kingdom of God in our generation.

Available at www.DrRobReimer.com

# Soul Care

## *7 Transformational Principles for a Healthy Soul*

*Soul Care* explores seven principles that can lead to lasting transformation and freedom for all who struggle with a broken, damaged, and sin-stained soul.

Brokenness grasps for the soul of humanity. We are broken body, soul, and spirit, and we need the healing touch of Jesus. *Soul Care* explores seven principles that are profound healing tools of God: securing your identity, repentance, breaking family sin patterns, forgiving others, healing wounds, overcoming fears, and deliverance.

Dr. Rob Reimer challenges readers to engage in an interactive, roll-up-your-sleeves and get messy process—a journey of self-reflection, Holy Spirit inspiration, deep wrestling, and surrender. It is a process of discovering yourself in true community and discovering God as He pierces through the layers of your heart.

Life change is hard. But these principles, when packaged together and lived out, can lead to lasting transformation, freedom, and a healthy soul. *Soul Care* encourages you to gather a small group of comrades in arms, read and process together, open your souls to one another, access the presence and power of God together, and journey together into the freedom and fullness of Christ.

# Soul Care Leader

## *Healthy Living and Leading*

How do we live a healthy life and lead others into spiritual, emotional and relational health and wholeness?

That is the focus of this book.

Trying to help others find freedom and wholeness is draining work. What do we do to become healthy and maintain our well-being? What are the practices and rhythms we need to engage in to be effective Soul Care practitioners? How do we create a culture where life-change flourishes? How do we minister in the power of the Spirit so that we can lead others into breakthroughs?

Too often people are talking about the same problems that they were talking about several years ago but they aren't finding a path to freedom. We need to help people get to the roots and not merely manage their dysfunction and sin. These are the questions and topics that this book will seek to equip you in as you seek to live and lead people into freedom and fullness in Christ.